# START THE
# PRESSES!

# START THE PRESSES!

## A HANDBOOK FOR STUDENT JOURNALISTS

FOREWORD BY
WILLIAM F. BUCKLEY JR.

**EDITOR**
Stanley K. Ridgley, Ph.D.

**SENIOR EDITORS**
Wesley David Wynne
Brent Tantillo

**ASSOCIATE EDITORS**
Winfield J. C. Myers
Thor Halvorssen
Alexandra Gilman
Tony Mecia

Revised and updated from a work by Aaron Barnhart.

ISI Books
Wilmington, Delaware

*Cataloging-in-Publication Data*

Start the presses!: a handbook for student
        journalists / foreword by William F. Buckley
        Jr.; edited by Stanley K. Ridgley. —1st ed.
        —Wilmington, DE : ISI Books, 2000

        p. ; cm.
        ISBN 1-882926-52-8
        1. Journalism, School. I. Ridgley,
        Stanley K. 1955- II. Buckley, William F. (William
        Frank), 1925-


LB3621 .S73 2000          00-100081
371/.897--dc21                    CIP

Printed in Canada by: Transcontinental Printing

ISI Books                         371.897 S897r
P.O. Box 4431
Wilmington, DE 19807-0431
www.isi.org
                                  Start the presses!

Cover art by Glenn K. Pierce.
Book design by Wesley David Wynne.

# CONTENTS

# FOREWORD

If a half century ago (I was a college editor in 1949) I had thought it conceivable that there would be an appetite for lore on publishing right-minded student papers at the turn of the century, I think I'd have abandoned my afflatus and gone sailing for the rest of my life. It happened that I was the editor of the *Yale Daily News.* In the course of my tenure as such, I established relations with what I gathered was the whole of the conservative community in the *Harvard Crimson* and the *Princetonian*: one student each. The progress has been pretty gratifying. What eludes us yet, of course, is épaté-ing the nonbourgeois editors of the institutional student papers. On the other hand, maybe that's not what we want. If the aspirant editor of the *Dartmouth Review* were to find himself elected editor of the *Dartmouth*, would we want to see the *Review* evaporate? I should think not.

The student conservative papers, in my experience—which is nonsystematic—do more than the regular student paper can do, much more. The student conservative papers have what I call a harnessing bias: a sense of a desirable order of things, and this requires more than what was at my disposal at Yale, which was simply the editorial page. A great use can be made of it, but to have the entire paper at one's disposal hugely enlarges the horizon, giving student writers a lot of windows, useful not only in passing along the word, and the perspective, but useful also in developing the student's skills as a writer and observer.

The handbook here prepared by ISI is a superb aid to useful thought and organization. Stanley Ridgley's very bright idea of reproducing individual essays from college papers pointing to this or another problem of the kind student papers come upon is a wonderful use of highly relevant material. How was this problem faced, or solved, or—unsolved? It is a major contribution to an intelligent use of time and a sophisticated allocation of resources.

The student publication world suffers from a single and absolutely unconquerable problem. It is that tomorrow's golden boy—who has a sure touch as an editorial writer, attracts other young writers, deftly allocates business responsibilities to a colleague, and spends time encouraging potential patrons among the alumni—graduates at the end of the year. A successor needs to winnow his or her way in. But even if the successor is ultimately successful, there is a hole left, hard to repair. Imagine the situation in the robust papers and magazines of the country if the editor in chief were permitted only a single term, and on the understanding that no junior editor could have spent more than two years in the trade.

But how does one guard against a contingency that can't be made to go away? In the seventies, returning to the University of Colorado for a lecture, I was surprised to find myself talking to the editor of the student daily, who I thought had a familiar face. Indeed he had—he had interviewed me seven years earlier. He was a committed leftist who, in behalf of his cause, kept postponing his graduation, by one or another device. This left him in charge of the student daily for two undergraduate generations. A committed man, but I note that Mr. Ridgley nowhere, in his readable book, recommends this course of action, even for the most fervent advocate of our cause, even with the most fervent loyalty to the college attended. If the University of Colorado had begun a tradition, we'd need something like the 25th Amendment to apply to student journalists.

One thing you'll notice, those of you who decide to engage in the delirious experience of journalism. It is that in college you will attract more attention than at any time, in any other situation in the future, unless you become president of the United States. A student journal can expect to be read by very nearly everybody.

It is a fine thing, to know that what you are thinking and saying will be reviewed by so many others. Not reverently, not thoughtfully, not sympathetically, in most cases. But it is fine to know that the words you elect to use, in the form you elect to use them, pointed at a direction you wish to go—are tomorrow's public property.

This wonderful manual, courtesy of ISI, is in the nature of a provisioning ship. You are naked and have elected to walk right across Antarctica. What do you do now?

You read *Start the Presses!* and sally forth, fully clothed, armored, equipped, oriented, and raring to go.

Bon voyage.

**William F. Buckley Jr.**
New York, NY

# Introduction

The modern conservative college press movement was launched in 1951, when twenty-five-year-old William F. Buckley Jr. had his first book published. *God and Man at Yale*, or *GAMAY* as it has become known, convulsed America's liberal academic community like no other book before or since. A trenchant critique of the secularization and collectivization of the Yale University ethos, *GAMAY* was likened to a totalitarian tract by liberal commentators unaccustomed to dealing with genuine difference of opinion. Mr. Buckley captured the spirit of the time—and the spirit of our own time as well—as he roasted the university's sacred cows on the spit of logic, style, and wit.

Mr. Buckley inspired an entire generation of young conservative activists, journalists, and intellectuals who went on to found college newspapers or who chose to work for campus dailies. With the active sponsorship or approval of the Intercollegiate Studies Institute (ISI), of which Mr. Buckley was the first president, papers were launched in the 1960s at Berkeley, Brown, Chicago, Columbia, Cornell, Harvard, Indiana, Northwestern, Pennsylvania, Villanova, Washington & Lee, Wisconsin, Yale, and other schools. These papers—*Man and State* (Berkeley), *Comment and Outlook* (Brown), *New Individualist Review* (Chicago), *Gentlemen of the Right* (Cornell), *The Harvard Conservative*, *The Alternative* (Indiana), *The Optimate* (Northwestern), *Analysis* (Penn), *Libertas* (Villanova), *The Southern Conservative* (Washington & Lee), *Insight and Outlook* (Wisconsin), and *The Alternative* (Yale)—formed the first network of campus newspapers. It was the golden age of conservative student journalism, and it was the young college journalists of the sixties who successfully battled the New Left radicals of that sorry decade.

The silver age of conservative college journalism began in 1979 with the founding of *Counterpoint* at the University of Chicago. John Podhoretz, a columnist at the *New York Post*, and Tod Lindberg, now editor of *Policy Review*, launched the newspaper which would be the first of a new organization of publi-

XII ■ START THE PRESSES!

cations—the Collegiate Network (CN) of conservative campus newspapers.

This group of papers burgeoned on America's campuses in the 1980s, a time when conservatism enjoyed a national resurgence under President Ronald Reagan. The CN was then administered by the Institute for Educational Affairs (IEA) under the direction of the neoconservative intellectual Irving Kristol, the great conservative patron William E. Simon, a former secretary of the treasury, and think-tank *wunderkind* Michael Joyce. IEA worked closely with the historic patron of student writing, ISI, to bring the finest intellectual and journalism training to the young conservatives of the time. The fruits of this training included papers like the famous *Dartmouth Review*, which produced journalists like Dinesh D'Souza and Laura Ingraham; the *Illini Review* at Illinois, which produced media critic Terry Teachout and author Michael Fumento; the *Yale Political Monthly*, which produced columnist Maggie Gallagher and *Foreign Affairs* editor Fareed Zakaria; and the *Michigan Review*, which produced *National Review* reporter John Miller and *Heterodoxy* reporter Benjamin Kepple.

The Collegiate Network, the home of college conservative journalism, is stronger than ever as it enters its third decade with a membership that exceeds seventy newspapers and journals nationwide. ISI, with almost a half century of stewardship of conservative student journalism behind it, is again guiding the nation's conservative college newspapers. As it has done since 1953, ISI trains successive generations of college students in the fundamentals of journalism as well as in the intellectual roots of the Western intellectual, political, and cultural heritage. Newspapers come and go, with new publications replacing those whose time is spent, but the students are the ultimate beneficiaries of college journalism. Because of their experience, they graduate well-rounded, humanely educated, and ready for the challenges facing America in the new century. And the spirit and élan of student editors remain the same as that inspired by William F. Buckley Jr. fifty years ago.

Mr. Buckley has been gracious to pen the foreword to this edition. It is fitting that he has done so, as he embodies the spirit of conservative student journalism in America. Perhaps no other person has inspired so many young people to an intelligent, thoughtful, self-regarding conservatism that exalts individual liberty against the nostrums of collectivists who continue to labor on the American campus, even now, so indefatigably.

As I consider the talented young journalists practicing their craft on the campus today, I am persuaded that an august new age of student journalism is upon us. In that spirit, I am confident Mr. Buckley's words will inspire, as they have done in the past, a new generation of young writers—the thinkers, opinion leaders, and shapers of America's future.

I hope that our efforts here on behalf of a fair, unbiased, and principled press, which believes that moderation in the pursuit of justice is no virtue, bears fruit across the land. For this handbook is a tool, useful only to the extent that the advice distilled here is put into action. Go forth, prosper...and *Start the Presses!*

**Stanley K. Ridgley, Ph.D.**
Wilmington, Delaware

# 1. Why Start a Campus Publication?

"DO I REALLY want to start my own publication?" The answer depends on what you want to accomplish. The number of approaches to alternative journalism is almost as great as the number of publications. All of them, however, to one degree or another affirm the following fundamental ideas:

◆ They want to counter the dominance, often unquestioned except by them, of the on-campus left-wing orthodoxy, whether it is housed in the administrative building, the classrooms, student government, the offices of the establishment campus newspaper, or all of the foregoing. They want to show that some people on campus still fight for and believe in freedom, truth, merit, the pursuit of excellence, and the immense contribution of the Western intellectual heritage.

◆ They want to gain a wide readership, especially among students who do not otherwise encounter conservative points of view.

◆ Student editors want to develop their journalistic skills in the friendly yet challenging environment of their own enterprise, where the ideological climate will not interfere with their commitment to excellence. This environment is often the only place on campus in which to do this.

## More Questions

No doubt you have other questions of a practical nature—not just the why, but the who, what, where, and when of publishing as well. Below are some of the most common questions that student editors ask the Collegiate Network. Our answers are not intended to be final, but simply give an idea of the investment of money and labor that an alternative publication requires.

## How much money will this cost?

The most inexpensive publications in the Collegiate Network cost about $800 per issue for 5,000 copies, including postage, production, and distribution costs. Without exception, these publications are printed on newsprint, the cheapest paper available (although many will spend $100 or so for the use of color on the cover). Start-up costs will run about $600 for software and occasional expenses like an office telephone, stationery, and production supplies. These expenses amount to roughly $600 per academic year. Computer costs can be high, but they vary widely depending on what resources are available to you. Most schools have personal computer labs for student use, in addition to whatever computers your staff may own. It is possible that all the programs you need to publish are already available—either you own them or you can use them at the computer lab, in which case your total investment for hardware and software is nothing. (The subject of desktop publishing is discussed more fully in the chapter "Publishing Topics.") Keep in mind that grant money may be available once you have published your first issue. (The subject of Collegiate Network grants is discussed in the chapter "Second Steps.")

## How often should we publish?

That's entirely up to you. But aim for eventually having at least a monthly schedule (six or eight issues per academic year). If you have the staff resources for it and think you can raise the money, consider starting up as a monthly. Many papers have done so. Papers published less frequently than every month run the risk of an "invisibility factor." They have a hard time getting regular readers, and the question their editors are most often asked is, "Did you guys go out of business?"

You must determine just the right balance of quality and quantity, an issue that you and your successors will grapple with for years to come. Publishing at the highest frequency and circulation your staff and finances permit, while filling a modest number of pages with consistently high-quality journalism, maximizes your visibility and impact on campus.

## WHAT TOPICS SHOULD WE WRITE ON? SHOULD IT BE ALL POLITICAL? WHO WILL WRITE FOR THE PUBLICATION? SHOULD WE ALLOW OPPOSING VIEWPOINTS ON OUR PAGES?

Questions of content are usually best answered by looking hard at the composite picture of your classmates. These people are your potential readership. Many of your classmates will pick up an issue mostly to check out any nonpolitical, nonintellectual writing. This group should not dictate your editorial policy, but you should pique their interest in your publication. Writing local, nonpolitical stories, as a supplement to your harder-hitting editorial fare, is a way to attract readers.

The chapter "A Story Seminar" shows how to find interesting stories on your campus. In the course of publishing your paper and gaining visibility among students, you will attract volunteer writers. These new writers will broaden your base on campus and give you an endless supply of story ideas.

## WILL WE GET IN TROUBLE WITH THE SCHOOL FOR STARTING UP OUR OWN PUBLICATION? DO WE HAVE RECOURSE IF SOMETHING HAPPENS?

You never know how the administration of a school that has not had alternative journalism on its campus will react to it. But as long as you do not break any libel laws and are willing to follow the distribution guidelines set by the school, you are not guilty of violating anything other than the sensitivities of people at your school who are used to having things *their* way. Even if the administration (or faculty or student government) throws obstacles in your way, you have a powerful defense: your creativity. Because even the smallest college must operate within a bureaucracy, it is possible for you to stay one step ahead of the regulators just by using your wits. If the "establishment newspaper" is allowed to put issues in special distribution bins at central locations or in student mailboxes, and yours isn't, you can drop your copies in places where distribution isn't *disapproved,* if not exactly approved—such as on the floor next to the "official" paper's bins or in the lobbies of student dorms and cafeterias. You may have to perform surveillance on your issues to ensure that a surly custodian or professor or student doesn't throw them out, and you must ensure that the issues are within sight of passersby. But the trouble is worth it if you can get the issue out without legal recourse. (Also see the discussion of the double standard in "A Story Seminar.")

## Do we need tax-exempt status?

You have three options. One is to file for IRS recognition as an independent, not-for-profit educational organization under Article 501(c)(3) of the revenue code. Here a *pro bono* lawyer will help. This is an attractive option, because it gives you complete financial independence from the university, but it also requires you to keep up the paperwork year after year.

A second option is to become recognized as a student organization at your school. You should consider doing this anyway, because as an official group you may be able to get privileges in the student union such as office space and perhaps even student government funds. And as an official student group, you could claim tax-exempt status under the university's nonprofit umbrella. However, there are almost always strings attached. You might be required to keep your finances with the university. You certainly run at least the risk of having your finances frozen or distribution outlawed at the whims of student government or an unfriendly administrator. This makes for great copy and is nothing you can't overcome. But if you believe the official climate would be hostile to your publication, you might be better off, like the *Duke Review*, as a "completely unofficial" student enterprise.

Finally, you can simply exist as an independent student publication without tax-exempt status. Sympathetic alumni still contribute to your paper, since they do so out of loyalty, not to get a tax break. This course of action keeps you off the IRS radar screen and avoids unnecessary and potentially troublesome legalities as well.

# WHY START A PAPER?

**By Morgan N. Knull**
Founder, *Wabash Commentary*

The appropriately self-styled "deconstructionists" populating university faculties may deny it, but words have meaning. And impact.

That's why alternative publications offer a compelling and contagious way to champion conservative ideas and opinions. Indeed, the history of political and social movements attests to the power of the written word, not only in achieving short-term objectives but in establishing and nurturing support for long-term victories.

Consider the work of Sam Adams and the colonial Committees of Correspondence. In the years before the Liberty Bell sounded a call to arms, patriots flooded newspapers and town squares with pleas for independence, sparking debate and influencing public opinion. They planted the philosophical roots for the United States.

Often the enduring impact of ideas is confirmed by the desperate measures that authorities employ to silence them. For instance, the publication of dissident Alexander Solzhenitsyn's *Gulag Archipelago*, which painstakingly documented the Soviet regime's horrific concentration camp system, so enraged authorities—even as, or perhaps because, it changed minds in the West—that he was expelled abruptly in 1974 from his own country. Yet this bestowed even greater fame on Solzhenitsyn.

During the first year of its publication, a founder of the *Dartmouth Review* was assaulted and bitten in the chest by an administrator attempting to block the paper's distribution. Though sent to the hospital for multiple stitches, Ben Hart and his staff persisted in dropping stacks of the *Review* about campus. When Dartmouth faculty later voted almost unanimously to condemn Hart for the incident, alumni and observers were outraged by the hostility shown toward free speech, let alone student safety.

The *Review* is just one success story in the phenomenon of alternative, independent campus publications. In 1994 students at Yale publishing *Light and Truth* exposed that university's deliberate misuse of a $20 million grant intended to promote the study of Western civilization. Dissatisfied with the administration's excuses, the donor, who previously had no reason to suspect the thwarting of his intentions, demanded a refund.

In recent decades, more than one hundred alternative campus publications have sprouted across the United States. Many are established from scratch; others begin as political club newsletters or philosophical journals and evolve into campus-oriented publications. You find a rich variety of styles and editorial positions among CN members.

While campus publications, as with any noble cause, require time commitment and determination, they are tremendously rewarding and effective. They demand accountability on campuses where faculty radicals too often run unleashed, but conservative students are muzzled. CN papers aren't afraid to tell the truth, and, in fact, there is no reason your college or university cannot have a CN paper. There are probably many reasons why it should.

"You will make all kinds of mistakes; but as long as you are generous and true, and also fierce, you cannot hurt the world or even seriously distress her," Winston Churchill once said. "She was made to be wooed and won by youth."

Campus leftists often accuse conservatives of creating a chilling effect on free speech, even though it is no secret that speech codes, sexual harassment policies, and pseudo-judicial inquisitions—the real threats to free speech—are promoted by those same leftists. Conservatives simply demand accountability and public scrutiny, believing that these complement genuine academic freedom. Independent papers serve as the conscience of schools, the guardian of traditions, and the voice of reason amidst the rot of higher education. They serve several purposes:

◆ Free from faculty and administrative censorship and restrictions, CN papers report news and provide commentary on subjects relevant to campus, with good prose, wit, and style.

◆ CN publications are highly visible, which helps recruit new staff and provides an ideal medium for persuading the indifferent and engaging the liberal.

◆ Offering tangible proof of conservative campus activism, publications earn devoted alumni subscribers and donors. Advertising also is a means of generating revenue.

◆ As part of an established network, CN editors build contacts and develop job skills for life after college. Some earn prestigious summer internships with publications and policy groups.

If starting a publication seems like a daunting challenge, it is. Staff recruitment, fundraising, writing and editing, layout and design, printing and distribution are necessary—and that's just to publish the first issue. Campus leftists harass you, faculty denounce you, and most students don't seem to notice or care.

Why start a publication? Why persist? Actually, most people wouldn't. Edmund Burke was fond of observing that evil triumphs because good men do nothing to oppose it. That's what makes CN editors and publications extraordinary.

Independent papers attract students who have fire in their bellies and quills in their hands. They are outraged at the moral cowardice of faculty, abhor the erosion of critical standards, and know that political slogans are a poor substitute for education. These young warriors oppose the conceit of administrators who attempt to return the campus to an era of *in loco parentis* and treat students not as free, independent minds but as their charges, as children in need of enlightenment from what administrators see as a sexist, racist, homophobic society. Far from being intimidated when confronted with attempts to silence them, they likely will respond by taking the story to the network evening news. Around campus, they acquire what is known as "a reputation," and they're proud of it.

The experience gained while working on a conservative paper is rewarding, formative, and memorable. You meet interesting people, probe and develop your own beliefs, refine your writing and speaking, and enjoy staff camaraderie. In the end, you may achieve some victories. Independent papers are for those with a reputation—for being passionate about truth.

# 2. First Steps

YOU'VE DECIDED to start a paper on your campus. You've decided it's worth the financial risk and you plan to raise the money through the student government, alumni donations, advertising, your parents, the Collegiate Network, or all of the above. Your next questions then are: How do I get the paper off the ground, besides gathering stories? What resources—at a bare minimum—do I need? Let's start at the beginning.

## Name and Mission

Your publication needs a name. The name should reflect the fact that it is a newspaper produced for your campus. The use of "Commentary," "Spectator," "Review," "Observer," "Criterion," "Independent," and "Free Press" are common. Obvious examples of publications that indicate their location are the *Stanford Review, Duke Review, Princeton Tory,* and *Harvard Salient.* However, your paper's title need not be tied to the name of the school. The *Primary Source* at Tufts and the *Fountainhead* at the University of Oklahoma are examples. The *Sewanee Legacy* at University of the South appeals to the traditions of the school.

It shouldn't be difficult to come up with a name, but it is important. You should feel comfortable with it. It must resonate. Remember that the name may be useful when introducing yourself on the telephone: "California Review" sounds more professional and mainstream than "Orthodox Inquisitor" or "Redwood Revolutionary." From an advertising perspective, the same consideration applies. Keep your fire for your content. The name should be appealing and benign— something that won't prevent passersby from picking up the paper.

Once you have a name, you should write a constitution for your publication. You may have to do this if you choose to become an official student group. Along with the constitution, you should reflect on what you wish to accomplish with your publication and invest time in writing a mission statement. This is your philosophical mantra, your Rock of Gibraltar in times of trouble. What do you stand for? How does your publication want to define itself?

The most successful Collegiate Network publications have well-written, dignified mission statements they publish in a certain space in *every* issue. This also serves as a tool for recruitment. Students will find the mission statement an enlightening explanation as to why you exist.

## STAFF

Once you have a mission you will need people. Loyal, reliable, hardworking people.

Two types of students join an alternative publication: "visionaries" and "productivity types." Every staff has a number of intellectually and politically motivated people—the visionaries. They will set and maintain the philosophical tone of your publication as writers and as editors. But some intellectually gifted writers are poor ad salesmen. Others make poor editors because they can't delegate duties or manage staff members. That is why alternative papers usually have in their leadership one or two persons who apparently have little interest in "the issues," but who have technical or interpersonal gifts that can move mountains under a deadline.

Also, assuming you want to attract readers who do not take an interest in political or intellectual affairs, your publication depends on journalists who write about campus life and culture to attract these readers. All of these people may be said to be productivity types—people who transform the mission of the visionaries into reality.

Your challenge is to recruit staff who can shoulder the practical load of everyday publishing while preserving the ideals of the publication. Recruiting and delegating duties to a staff is also a matter of maintaining your balance.

To be effective you must not only have a good staff mix, but you must also delegate major responsibilities to more than one or two people. Uneven division of labor puts an unnecessary burden on a few while leaving the rest with little to do. An all-powerful editor may be preoccupied with news and opinions, for instance, and may allow the other sections to go stale from neglect. He can neither recruit new writers nor sell ads. And it is likely that no one will permanently assume the chore of layout in such a situation. This could throw your publication's appearance into chaos.

Divide labor sensibly. Establish a leadership structure with posts such as editor, publisher, and managing editor. If you don't do it now, you'll have to do it later when you're recruiting your successors. What follows is a suggested structure of staff roles and responsibilities. Take it as a guide only.

◆ An editor in chief should manage all aspects of the publication except the financial aspects. He assigns and collects all stories for all sections; edits and proofs all copy; and determines all story-related artwork, including pictures, graphics, headlines, and captions. This is a task of supervision. In order to perform it well and leave adequate time for thinking about stories, he should appoint a managing editor as his right hand.

◆ The editor in chief should have a production chief and subeditors for each major section (news, opinion, features).

◆ A publisher manages all financial matters, including advertising, fundraising, and bookkeeping. He should probably conduct the latter two functions himself and recruit an advertising staff with its own manager to handle the first.

## RECRUITMENT

Long-term survival for an independent publication means recruiting constantly. Recruitment pays short- and long-term dividends: in the short term it relieves the leadership of having to perform all the tasks of the publication; in the long run, it fattens up the staff box you print on page two and gives everyone the sense of working on a stable, successful project.

Students join independent publications for myriad reasons, and they bring with them new ideas for stories. Some may write columns or cover beats you hadn't thought of. New volunteers represent a net gain in the number of man-hours put into each issue, provided you know how to use them properly.

The recruitment process involves two steps: casting lures and reeling in people. Your campus is a lot better stocked than most streams. First, however, you must know how to fish.

## Casting Lures

Some recruitment tactics are more effective than others. One tactic that always works is to publish "house advertisements" in every issue; a quarter-page ad in the *Kenyon Observer* says simply, "Write for the *Kenyon Observer*. E-mail: sterlingc@kenyon.edu." A full-page ad in the *Red and Blue* at the politically charged University of Pennsylvania features a picture of Mel Gibson's Scottish hero William Wallace charging into battle. The caption reads: "They may take our tuition, but they'll never take our freedom....We are looking for a few good men and women to join the staff of Penn's most controversial student publication. If you think you have what it takes to become one of us, call Dave at 573-5555." These ads pull in readers who like your publication. Provide them a phone number or e-mail address to contact immediately and, if you have an office, invite them to visit.

The best way to recruit students by means of your paper is to publish a summer issue and mail it to the homes of incoming students. Three or four people can assemble it by combining a few first-rate stories published during the previous year along with some new articles. You should plan a social for orientation week and run a full-page advertisement for it during the summer, so that new students may meet the editors of your publication. Promote the event with flyers around campus as well. At the social, provide forms for interested students to fill out, and follow up with phone calls to get them involved.

Remember, you offer something no other outfit on campus can—a chance to get your name in print, fast. The daily, with its oppressive bureaucratic structure and with dozens of staffers, can't promise that. Your smallness and accessibility, and the fact that you produce regular results (that can be clipped and attached to résumés), will attract a wide variety of students. You can't predict who joins or why, but they *will* join if you publicize.

If you print your first issue in the middle of the academic year, consider holding a mixer shortly thereafter. The *Wabash Commentary* made a splash when it was founded at Wabash College. To let students know that *Commentary* editors were not the monsters depicted by the administration and their student minions, they regularly held social events and even executive breakfasts. This served to publicize the paper and to recruit staff. It gave the *Commentary* cachet. Be sure your staff meets regularly enough that you can get recruits involved as soon as possible after they call you. If you don't, they will join some other group that's more reliable.

## REELING THEM IN

Once you have interested a student in your paper, follow up immediately. If you don't hear from a regular staffer for a couple of weeks, you usually don't worry. But when you reel in a new recruit, you want to stay in close contact with him, until he has some clips and feels like a regular. Give him an assignment interesting enough that he doesn't decide early on it's not worth the trouble. Your enterprise is small enough that there is always something somebody can do that conveys importance and real responsibility. All jobs are vital to the paper; no one knows that better than you. You must transmit this fact to your recruits frequently.

Bringing new staff aboard is a task for everyone in leadership positions. Still, you may want to appoint someone as your "new staff editor" to concentrate on giving assignments to recent recruits and to work with them until they are in print. Move away from doing all the nonwriting tasks yourself. If you are short of production people, for instance, you may find that a simple advertisement in your paper will attract a volunteer who wants to learn production.

What about more pesky tasks, like bulk-mailing issues to subscribers? Or manning the office phone to maintain office hours? Perhaps you can roll several small tasks into a single job description and find a volunteer to fill it. Or you might find, just by asking each new recruit, that many of your writers would be willing to shoulder an additional small nonwriting chore.

Whatever it takes, try to avoid burdening any one person in your leadership with too many tasks. That way, they can better concentrate on performing their main duties.

# How to Start: The Amherst Experience

**By Ross Cohen**
Former Editor, *Amherst Spectator*

In 1997, I reestablished the defunct *Amherst Spectator*, a conservative magazine at Amherst College. Initially, we had anticipated producing an eight-page magazine every two months with a staff of three or four. However, by the first distribution date, we had a monthly twenty-four-page magazine with a staff of twenty.

If you are considering starting a conservative magazine on your campus, you are probably overwhelmed, discouraged, and even confused by the numerous and seemingly insurmountable obstacles confronting your start-up and operation.

In this article, I unravel the mystery of starting and running a publication by sharing with you the specifics behind our success story.

## The Beginning

To guide your efforts and build a committed staff, the first step is to define your goals. Why are you starting the magazine? What role do you expect it to play on campus? What good do you envision the magazine doing? Answer these questions and set clear objectives and a vision for your project by writing a mission statement.

Find out the procedure for establishing your magazine as an official campus organization at your school. This process should be outlined in your school's student handbook. Official recognition provides a wide range of benefits. At Amherst it entitles groups to use school computers and to petition for student activities money; however, it often requires cutting through red tape. Leave plenty of time on your calendar for a barrage of administrative work. Start by obtaining a campus mailbox and e-mail address.

A good deal of your early efforts involve identifying and securing resources, including printing services, computer time, money, and talent. You should jump on these chores early, then follow through on them continuously.

When looking for a printer, try to learn about the industry.

Talk to as many printers as possible and be sure to ask technical questions. You can apply this knowledge to improve the appearance of your layout and to leverage a better price. Printing will be your biggest cost—don't pay more than you have to.

Computer time, on the other hand, should be free. Some schools provide special publications rooms, and almost all schools have computer centers, complete with PageMaker, Photoshop, scanners, high resolution printers, and other essential tools.

The first rule of financing a magazine is that you can never have too much money; printing is expensive and the quality of materials can always be upgraded. At the *Spectator*, we sell subscriptions to alumni, solicit advertising from local businesses, and have obtained student activities funds and Collegiate Network grants to meet our budgetary needs. Because the advertising market is competitive, we offer bulk rate deals to advertisers and pay high commissions to our salespeople. It is best to diversify your revenue sources to avoid becoming overly reliant on any one source. You should also open a bank account. Look for a bank with special rates for nonprofit organizations; our account is free.

Finally, you must recruit and manage a staff. People with publishing knowledge are extremely useful to a start-up, but enthusiasm can substitute. Arrange for experienced staff to train novices. Capitalize on the fact that the magazine is new; emphasize the room for creative input provided by a start-up magazine.

## Generating Interest

The size of your school and existing resources determine your approach to recruiting. Amherst is a small school with no clearly defined network for identifying conservative students. In this case, a word-of-mouth campaign, coupled with telephone networking, was successful. I also employed mass media techniques; I displayed posters in the campus center and put out table tents in the cafeteria explaining the magazine's mission and advertising the introductory meeting.

Were Amherst a larger or less liberally oriented institution, I would have advertised in a daily newspaper or recruited at a

Republican club, neither of which exist on campus. Consider your school's existing extracurricular structure and utilize those unique characteristics.

Establish face-to-face contact with students to ensure that you attract a number of interested people to your first meeting.

## THE FIRST MEETING

A lot rides on the success of the inaugural meeting. Strong attendance and a sense of leadership and commitment are critical. Successful recruiting methods will secure the former, but you must work to establish the latter.

Before the meeting, create a handout for distribution. Include background on the magazine, your mission statement, a production schedule, and an agenda for the meeting. Print the handout on magazine letterhead.

The production schedule on the handout should specify due dates and milestones. Outline all the major steps of production, including story deadlines, photography deadlines, meetings, and the actual layout. Set aggressive, yet realistic dates, and leave some room for slack.

Also, begin identifying interested students suited for leadership positions and develop an organizational structure. Early on, you will need a publisher to manage finances, a production chief to design and supervise layout, and a managing editor to assign and oversee content; but save a few leadership positions for later recruits.

At the meeting, maintain a strong focus and sense of purpose. Keep the meeting well organized and brief, and stick to the agenda. Be prepared to demonstrate the need for the magazine. For example, in the *Spectator's* first meeting, I used a copy of the student newspaper to discuss the weekly news. I spoke about events that the paper omitted, pointed out obvious liberal bias, and explained how our magazine would have approached the news differently.

The success of the first meeting will convey a sense of focus, commitment, and leadership that will attract people and give them confidence in the project. You want prospective staff to see that your magazine is a well-run organization that will succeed in putting out a top-notch product.

## FROM IDEA TO PRODUCT

Before assembling the first issue, develop a layout template. Take ideas from other campus or even national magazines, but keep your initial design simple to minimize problems. A good template will also include standard sections that appear in every issue to provide consistency and humor. The *Spectator* runs a satirical table-tent on the back cover and a parody as the centerfold each month.

Aim for diverse and balanced articles for your first issue and leave plenty of time for editing and revising them. Each issue of the magazine should have a unifying theme; the cover, special features, and some articles should relate to each other through this common link.

Well-placed, appropriate graphics add to the aesthetics and readability of the magazine. Identify the types of graphics to run with each story and their locations. You need an artist and a photographer to produce the images and a computer guru to digitize them.

As you assemble the work of numerous people into one cohesive product, it is essential to stay organized and on your timetable. Schedule weekly meetings to stay in constant contact with contributors, keep motivation and morale high, and establish accountability through constant communication.

Do all of this, and you will be on your way to a successful first issue.

# HOW TO START: THE WILLIAMS EXPERIENCE

**By Damon A. Vangelis**
Founder, *Williams Free Press*

My high school newspaper advisor was a walking and talking quotation machine. His favorite was: "Do not mess with the man who buys his ink by the barrel and his paper by the pound." And if that one didn't leave an impression upon our staff, a quote from Wilbur F. Story surely did: "The job of a newspaper is to print the news and raise hell."

My advisor was a sixties radical who often said with remorse, "We were so close. If only we could have 1968 to do over again. We could have won."

While I disagreed with my advisor's politics, we shared a common commitment to search for the truth, something which often is absent from college campuses these days.

Having spent part of two summers during high school at the Columbia School of Journalism, I had a basic understanding of how newspapers operated and had the confidence and interest to work with one when I entered Williams College. The only question for me was whether I would join the campus weekly or work within the conservative intellectual circle.

The conservatives gathered every Thursday for dinner to discuss politics and campus affairs at the James A. Garfield Republican Club (named in honor of the twentieth president and 1856 graduate of Williams). It was our version of the Solidarity Movement in the Gdansk shipyard. The club meetings were a time to learn from other club members, socialize with guest lecturers and professors, and build friendships with like-minded conservatives on a campus dominated by the apathetic and the twin towers of intellectual destruction—the limousine and phony liberals.

I was drawn to the concept of an alternative newspaper, free from administrative control or institutional pressure. I decided to link my background in journalism with my interest in the need for reform on the campus.

At the close of my sophomore year, I created a biweekly newspaper, the *Williams Free Press* (*WFP*). To support the effort,

I created a nonprofit 501(c)(3) educational foundation, which I named The Zenger Foundation in honor of John Peter Zenger, the colonial publisher accused of seditious libel by the British government. Zenger was acquitted by a jury that concluded that he could not be convicted because what he published was true, and his trial ushered in a tradition of a free press in America. Initial financial support came from parents and alumni who had subscribed to previous conservative publications. The Zenger Foundation provided the paper with the institutional support to ensure that it would not fizzle after the founders graduated. As alumni, they still have an interest in its success.

The *WFP* rivaled the campus weekly, which had never had competition, and also became the focal point for a renewed community-wide interest in the campus. After seven years of publication, the *WFP* had nearly 700 parent and alumni sub-scribers and a lively letters section. Often alumni copy the *WFP* on letters they send to the college president and trustees. Therefore, in addition to covering campus affairs, the paper is a powerful communication tool that links students and alumni.

The Williams' administration can no longer rely on spin control and its "all rosy" propaganda to fool the greater campus community into believing that all is well. The more an alterna-tive voice challenges the administration to be truthful, the more the students, the college, and the country benefit.

In addition to publishing a newspaper, the staff of the *WFP* also sponsors lectures, campus debates, and panel discussions on critical issues facing the college and higher education. By linking the themes in these events with issues covered in the newspaper, the paper effectively shapes the battle of ideas on campus.

Williams College, like many schools across the country, touts diversity in all matters racial, sexual, and geographical. Never a peep about true diversity, however—the diversity of ideas. At Williams, for example, in 1992, all but two members of the faculty (according to a campus poll) voted for Bill Clinton. Currently, there is not a single Republican in the economics or political science departments. Williams continues to raise record amounts of money from alumni, is regularly rated among the top three small colleges across the country by *U.S.*

*News and World Report,* and continues to attract top students. But it is doing so by living off its past.

The absence of intellectual diversity at Williams and other campuses is a serious cause for concern especially when there is a nationwide reconsideration of the "Great Society" and government-sponsored discrimination that goes by the name of "affirmative action." The gulf between the college campus and the rest of the country shortchanges students seeking a meaningful and well-rounded education. An alternative campus newspaper can be the first step toward bridging that gulf.

# Looking to the Future: It's Time to Recruit

**By Tony Mecia**
Former Program Director, Collegiate Network

Collegiate Network editors often complain they cannot recruit enough staff to produce a successful paper. We all know that running a newspaper is not easy. Ideally, there should be staff selling ads, writing articles, soliciting donations, coordinating distribution, editing, and laying out the paper.

Too often, however, those tasks fall on the shoulders of a dedicated few. Now is the time to recruit new staff members to your publication.

Developing a winning recruitment strategy reaps dividends in the long run; you can ensure division of labor throughout the year and also provide for your paper's success if you recruit and train new underclassmen.

As students know from experience, the first semester of the year is crucial for finding eager new members, particularly freshmen, for any campus organization. Freshmen enter the school year looking for new and exciting ways to broaden their college experiences. Your task is to find these people and sell them on your publication.

In the first weeks of school, the universities often provide forums during orientation for all campus organizations to set up booths and distribute materials. You should seize this opportunity to sign people up, then invite them to your paper's first meeting. It is helpful to have copies of your publication on your table so prospective staffers will know what to expect. Even if you missed your school's activities fair this year, you should consider setting up a booth in a well-traveled area of campus, such as the student center.

You should also heavily advertise your meetings. Post signs in well-travelled places around campus, or buy an ad in your school's main newspaper. If your newspaper can afford it, you should offer something that few college students can refuse— free food. Pizzas and Cokes at your meeting will draw students to you in droves.

Keep your meetings as fun, productive, and inclusive as possible. If you hold an enjoyable meeting, people will return. Psychology provides insight here: students attend your meeting because of their dedication to the cause, but many join your paper if working for it is fun. Many freshmen know only a few students their first several weeks, so they view joining a club as a way to meet people. To retain these newcomers, make your organization appealing. Hold a tailgate party before a football game, or a staff party on a Friday or Saturday night. Again, the principle of free food and drink applies. Such activities also allow you to know your staff better.

Your meetings should be productive. Talk about the status of your paper's current issue, assign tasks, and ask your current staff to report on their activities. Don't get bogged down with in-depth discussions that can better be held elsewhere and that will bore many of the newer recruits. Everyone likes a quick and efficient meeting; avoid two-hour marathons that accomplish little.

Involve new people in your meeting. Have them introduce themselves to the group and say why they became interested in your publication. Ask for their advice on important matters. Don't be critical or doctrinaire with them—you want them to return.

After the meeting, talk to the new people individually. At this stage, you can determine their specific interests. Keep in mind that you are not looking only for writers. Search for dedicated people who have strengths in business, ad sales, or layout.

You might find someone whose forte is not student journalism but event planning. A Director of Special Events can plan staff parties, schedule meetings with sympathetic faculty and potential donors, and bring lecturers to campus. Events like these strengthen your status as *the* conservative force on campus.

Attracting people to your paper, getting them involved—these are the challenges CN papers constantly face. With a solid recruiting strategy and plenty of personal contact, your publication can ensure its long-term success.

# 3. A Story Seminar

THE NEXT TWO CHAPTERS cover the tasks involved in publishing your first few issues. This chapter discusses editorial concerns, while in the next chapter we turn to business issues and your publication's design.

Think of the following as a class seminar on how to develop a story: from brainstorming and research to writing and editing. Other chapters discuss questions such as where the stories will go and how to dress them up so that they look inviting to read. For now, though, we consider the story—the single most important element in any publication and the key to success on your campus.

"The story" is any article that is timely and appropriate for your publication. The guidelines below were written to help you think not only about good stories for your front page, but also features, editorials, and reviews.

## Story Selection: Beats and Angles

Students who envision themselves as hard-hitting campus journalists and who want people to actually read their articles should adopt the following sentence as their editorial mantra: Focus on campus issues.

It's easy but ineffective to script articles about people and places far removed from the campus. It's tempting because you won't be ruffling the feathers of anyone you'll meet on the street—it's more difficult to write about living, breathing people you see every day. But campus-oriented articles are effective precisely *because* you are dealing with issues close to home.

This advice probably strikes some the wrong way—particularly those students who want to hold forth on national and international issues, who want to write about Congress or China or the national budget. Unfortunately, the hard truth is that faculty, your fellow students, and others who happen to read your paper don't want to read your opinions on those subjects. For that type of information they will go elsewhere—*Time, Newsweek,* or *U.S. News.*

Readers of your paper do not pick up the student newspaper to get information on national and international issues. They read it to find out what's happening at the college.

You can distinguish yourself by publishing well-researched exposés about the faculty, the administration, student government, the curriculum, or any of a dozen other areas ripe for exposure. *That* is how you become a player on campus, and that is how you can identify yourself as an important source of information for people outside your college. A great example of this type of journalistic start is William F. Buckley, Jr., who wrote the classic exposé of Yale University, *God and Man at Yale.* It became a bestseller and marked Buckley as an important thinker and talented writer.

If the young Yale grad had instead chosen to write about the Korean War, it's a good bet that his book never would have seen print. Instead, Buckley wrote about what he knew. He wrote about the secularization and collectivization of Yale's curriculum. Consequently, he wrote a book that no one outside the Yale campus was qualified to write, and one for which *he* was uniquely qualified.

You may hear different advice from your own faculty and administrators. They will probably encourage you to write on the "important issues of the day" because the world "needs to hear young, idealistic voices filled with fresh ideas." Or other such nonsense.

They say this, because they don't want you writing about *them.* Their advice, of course, is poppycock.

If you want to become a powerful student publication, you will write *for* the students of the little community that is your school. You must earn the reputation of being locally oriented, and you earn it through constant reinforcement in the minds of your readers. If students see an attention-getting headline on the front page on a topic that interests them, they will pick up the issue. If they read the stories and find them informative, well-written, and about *them,* it will confirm their first impressions and they will be much more likely to pick up the next issue. Soon, many readers will pick up your publication from habit.

Your job is to establish and maintain this reputation. Don't worry about national issues—unless they influence local affairs. Think of your job in terms of "beats" and "story angles." You may have a few "location beats" such as the administration building and student government. But you'll also have "idea beats" such as the college curriculum, faculty practices, and political issues. Organize your beats and assign reporters to them. When your reporters return with interesting topics, you spin out the best story angle for each and decide if it is worth pursuing.

Your beats should include student government, the student Left, the student Right, the administration, the faculty, and the identity-politics offices. Covering the first three is easy: assign a reporter to each group and have the reporters monitor each group's calendar of upcoming events. Attend as many events as possible. When conservative or libertarian groups host speakers, cover the events. Look for a local angle in their remarks and perhaps run an interview with the speaker (if he isn't boring). With government and the student Left, most of what you write is follow-up: reports on legislation or incidents involving the group that are newsworthy. ("Newsworthiness" will be determined by the angle you choose, as discussed below.) You may be unable to get into the meetings of the student Left, but you can certainly attend their rallies and read their literature.

Administration and faculty require a defter touch. Official events and publications are easy enough to monitor, but what's happening behind closed doors? What is the faculty senate talking about and voting on? Which departments bubble with controversy, and which quietly and effectively push their own radical agendas? Which are doing neither? How are they changing the curriculum? Where does the money go? To look into these two imposing structures, you need "eyes." These are provided by people who are inside those structures and who are willing to share with you their insights. Once you identify and contact friendly administrators and professors, assign a writer to stay in regular touch with them. Another method, discussed below, is to regularly read the official news of the school, as reported in the daily newspaper, alumni magazine, and minutes of important meetings. Look for the odd fact or eye-opening new development (usually buried deep in the official text).

In the last decade a new set of offices has appeared on campuses nationwide: they masquerade as "support" offices and "wellness" centers for special interests, but they in reality serve as havens for mediocre administrators who impose their philosophies of multiculturalism and moral relativism on unwitting students and who brook no criticism. Focus a keen eye on these offices and their personnel.

Professors and administrators may encourage you to stay away from "divisive" topics. They want you to write about national issues so you don't write about *them*. They don't want to see their names in your articles, and as long as you're writing opinion articles about national issues, they're safe.

Remove their safety net. Look closely at campus issues. Become an expert on the workings of your school. Write about the backroom deals, the bad food, affirmative action double standards, and zany courses.

As for stories that don't usually make the front page—sports, entertainment, other nonpolitical features—the more beats you have, the more material you generate each issue, thus the more selective and strategic you can be in choosing stories to run. Editors who do nothing but think up ideas and supervise other writers are essential to your publication. Each section should have one.

Have them collect more stories than you need, and you will acquire the freedom to run only the best.

## Story Angles

The local angle is two-sided.

This means searching both for good stories that are indigenous to your school and for relevant angles of certain national issues. To demonstrate the latter: Let's say a minority student organization on campus prints a declaration that most of the required courses in the area of literature are Eurocentric and insensitive toward the Third World. This is followed by a small demonstration and a meeting with the school's president. You report the events; you write an editorial critical of the group's stance. Then, six months later, who should come to town but the man who has built a career on the politics of poverty and minority issues—Jesse Jackson! Now which story is more likely to gain a student's interest: a profile of Jackson or an update on the curriculum story you ran earlier? You can run both stories. But since the establishment student newspaper will probably profile him too, your scoop will be to link the national figure—Jesse Jackson—to the local agitators and to show the weaknesses in their stances. If you profile Jackson, portray him not as the man the establishment newspaper *wants* him to be (their profile will no doubt speak of this "great leader") but as the man he actually is—a *provocateur.*

The staff of the *Stanford Review* has long known the importance of the local angle. When he was a student in the late eighties, Peter Thiel, the founder of the *Stanford Review,* hosted then-Secretary of Education William Bennett when Bennett arrived to persuade Stanford's faculty to retain its curriculum in Western civilization. The national coverage of the event convinced Thiel that stories should be local in focus and have a wider scope only as a bonus—not the other way around. "Indeed, the *Stanford Review* would have done better to avoid national and international issues entirely," he wrote later. "Such issues are worth coverage if they have local angles—if Oxfam uses money from student fasts to buy guns for the Sandinistas, for instance. But otherwise, off-campus issues are not appropriate topics for college newspapers. Those issues are already covered in other media, and they occupy space that could be devoted to local events. We have succeeded when we have run noneditorial, well-defined news pieces that focus on Stanford issues."

Sometimes the national stories don't come to your campus, but you can bring them there anyway. Once or twice every year a major book appears about an issue in higher education that has nothing in it about your particular school. Books such as Mary Lefkowitz's *Not Out of Africa* and Dinesh D'Souza's *Illiberal Education* are examples. Which story will be more newsworthy in the opinion of your classmates: an interview with the book's author (sometimes not very interesting and always difficult to obtain), a general review of the book, or a story about one of your school's departments being inspired by one of the chapters in the book? Obviously the last. You may not even have to cite the book or interview the author, but the book will help you gain more insight into your local situation and argue more effectively.

You can develop all sorts of stories using this second, "deductive" method, and often your best source of material will be the CN. One of the perks of Collegiate Network membership is that you can download stories from the CN Syndicate website. These stories come from other colleges and universities across the country. You can also link to their websites through the CN website and benefit from seeing their publications. Study them closely. What stories are effective? What angles did they take on particular issues?

What about topics that don't relate to any current national trend? You get to select the stories that are most newsworthy—an overused adjective in the journalism trade, to be sure, but one that takes on special significance for alternative journalists. The most common kinds of newsworthy stories are listed below.

◆ *Man bites dog.* Readers' eyes often glaze over ho-hum stories, but they focus suddenly on an unusual headline or a lead paragraph that provides unexpected facts. This is why investigative journalism is so popular. It takes things that the average reader pays little attention to—his drinking water, his breakfast cereal, his congressman—and reveals facts about them in such a way as to provoke responses.

When you think about it, this may well be your most productive and reliable story angle. The average student assumes that his school is devoted to the free exchange of ideas, and he expects professionalism from his administrators and professors. When one of these fundamental assumptions is violated, you have a story and a good angle on it. If a speaker's talk is interrupted by a radical activist, you could certainly write an opinion piece denouncing the violation of free speech. But the real story is man-bites-dog: public standards turned on their heads. If, for instance, a liberal professor is denounced as a racist, you will find that a news story is the better way to capture the situation's rich irony.

◆ *The dog that didn't bark.* Forming "beats" of the most prominent institutions on campus gives you a pipeline of regular
information from these sources. A great deal of it is unusable, of
course, because your competition has the same beats. But by
tapping into these sources, you can get a feel for how they
operate and where potential stories may lurk within them.

For instance, examine the size of the administration. Has the
president created scores of new positions during his tenure?
Why? Are they curriculum-related or special-interest-related? If
the former, what do the new administrators have to show for
their efforts over the past ten years? If the latter, what are the
special interests? How does the president's hiring practices
compare with those of his predecessor? With those of other
schools' presidents? How has the administrative side of your
school increased over the past ten years, and how does that
compare with the increase in the faculty?

◆ *Old wine in new wineskins.* If the details of the story are
already well known to most readers, the purpose instead is to
illuminate certain arguments that have been overlooked in other
write-ups of the subject.

A cover story in the October 1988 *Carolina Critic* targeted
the University of North Carolina's new mandatory food service
plan for on-campus students. There had been a change in
vendors, as everyone knew; what was less well known were the
effects that the new contract would have on students' freedom
of choice—and on their pocketbooks. The *Critic's* 1,500-word
story sought to change that by detailing the arrangement,
pointing out its most insidious aspects, and arguing against
them both from a libertarian perspective and from plain common sense. Students were going to be charged $100 per semes-
ter for food service meals, whether they used them or not. This
in turn created an unfair advantage for the food service over
local restaurants and a black market for unused meal tickets. In
short, it was an unconscionable bargaining tactic for the university to use to lure a food service contractor.

◆ *The interview.* Sometimes, an interview can run as a stand-
alone story. Of course, your subject must be significant; his
opinions must also be worth reading. And you should be timely.

If Newt Gingrich is to speak at your school, why not interview him one week earlier and time it so that your 2,000-word interview coincides with his speech? But don't limit your interview field to celebrities. You may want to devote a full story to the views of a leading intellectual or public official if he can give expert (and, hopefully, provocative) opinions on a topic that is news at your school. The interview could run as an accompanying article to an investigative story you are writing on the same topic.

◆ *The follow-up* (see the Jesse Jackson-visits-campus example, above). The average professional beat reporter will write at least one follow-up story for every new story he writes. Interesting topics have a way of getting readers' attention every time they show up in print. Writing follow-up stories can be an effective way of keeping on the front burner such broad, many-faceted topics as a controversial professor or a school policy you oppose. However, a follow-up story should appear genuinely fresh to its readers. Here's how to ensure that it is:

(1) *Find a brand-new "peg" on which to hang the follow-up story.* Was action promised on an issue when you ran the story last time? If action wasn't taken, there's your peg. If action happens, get on it and don't simply relate the news, because your competitor does that anyway, but add depth by showing how it is simply the latest development in an ongoing story you have reported previously.

(2) *Update the story thoroughly.* Before recycling old material, scan it carefully for any time-dated facts that may have changed since the original story was written. You can refer to the original, but don't quote from it verbatim. The best way to prepare for follow-ups is through the effective use of story files (discussed below). Much of the research that goes into any story winds up as background; i.e., it never actually sees print. But in refreshing your memory on your old notes and background interviews, you may decide that there is information in them that could be moved to the foreground. A newly relevant quote or a document you collected three months ago would be an example.

## PREPARATION

Research is essential to writing anything, be it a term paper, an editorial, or a story. Researching a story is vital because you are not only competing with other students and other viewpoints (leftists, liberals, even others on your own publication), but you are also racing the clock. You want an especially lean research arsenal containing a handful of effective techniques. When you decide on a story idea, your arsenal should be ready to help you produce a *complete story,* on *deadline.*

The best way to prepare for research is to *be organized,* in three ways especially: by using files, by monitoring other publications, and by filtering ideas prior to doing research.

◆ Begin collecting news stories into file folders that are labeled by topic for easy reference. For example, "Faculty," a broad topic, should have several folders, one each for the major (or most controversial) departments at your school, plus one titled "Faculty-Misc. Depts." Another folder contains official documentation, like the faculty lists of all departments (with credentials); another folder, with clippings of recent tenure cases; and so on. Then when you write a story on a topic, clip it and file it in a separate folder with all the reporter's notes (those that are legible). Add any follow-up stories to that folder. Just reading the folder labels every now and then will remind you of potential stories you once considered and that are worth doing now.

◆ Each editor of your publication should volunteer to monitor certain newspapers and journals, student internet newsgroups, departmental listservers, and, if available, the computer listservers of special interest groups. These are always good sources of new story ideas. Even though more than one of you may read the *New York Times,* for instance, one person should be responsible for reading it thoroughly every day and clipping relevant stories. Someone else should read everything in the establishment student paper, since most of you will want only to skim it most days. Also keep track of such publications as the *Chronicle of Higher Education* and ISI's *CAMPUS.* If you can't subscribe and tear out articles, make photocopies or at least keep a running list of stories that catch your eye. A brainstorming session at your writers' meeting is the parliamentary equivalent of "new business." Nobody just thinks up new business at a meeting; people bring agendas. If you take your thoughts to meetings in written form, you will increase your brainstorming power considerably.

◆ Be a filter for unusable story ideas. Remember, once you assign a story to a writer, you're not going to see it again until you are very close to your printer's deadline. So before you assign, you need to know what kind of story you want written. You should be able to tell early on—during the brainstorming session or before the writers' meeting even occurs—what kinds of stories you *don't* want written. Once you decide on a story, give the writer assigned to it an angle. By anticipating ways to pursue a story idea, you will know beforehand the reasons for or against each of the available story angles. Again, this means bringing a plan to the meeting rather than creating your agenda there. You can then do what meetings do best: turn good ideas into good stories—before a single word is written. Some CN papers have a harder edge than others. They tend to the satirical, in the finest tradition of H.L. Mencken or the *American Spectator*. The *Duke Review* has always tended to go for the belly laugh at some poor administrator's expense.

## General Rules

### For writers

First, some positive energy. The best single piece of writing advice I can offer is to buy and read two books: *The Elements of Style* by William Strunk and E. B. White, and *Write Tight* by William Brohaugh. Read them with care and attention, and then follow their counsel. Now, to the stories themselves.

The first rule of good writing, discussed above, is good preparation. Your stories should demonstrate an agility with the facts and arguments that comes only through good organization.

Assuming your publication has a thoughtful story strategy, the research and reporting you do should simply enable the facts to speak for themselves. Getting the facts requires several strong skills:

◆ *Determination.* This is known to media-watchers as aggressiveness. As much as we disdain the field of professional journalism for what is often simplistic thinking, we admire the way most reporters go about getting their stories. They are relentless. They do not take "No" for an answer from any bureaucrat, famous figure, or secretary. When they do get information, they ensure that all details are accurate, even if that means asking a source over and over to clarify and repeat what he said. When they find a useful article, they clip or photocopy it and refer to it frequently, so that they have a better feel for the topic overall. They are like Jonathan Winters in *It's a Mad, Mad, Mad, Mad World,* chasing every productive lead, grilling everyone around them for new information, until they wind up in just the right position to discover, not really by accident, that they are standing underneath the Big W. (Whether they possess the ability to write the best story possible from that wealth of research is another matter entirely.)

◆ *Timeliness.* This means finding a recent event that serves as the news "peg" for your story. But it also means getting the best possible version of the story in time for your next issue. Writers shouldn't file stories unless they believe they have accomplished what they set out to do. If this means missing a deadline, however, it is better to narrow the topic and submit a complete story. There will always be another issue in which the story can be continued as a follow-up or as the next installment. Likewise, editors need time to work on a writer's story; this means setting deadlines for stories that precede the printer's deadline by at least a few days.

A collection of tips follows, organized by subject matter. They come from the experiences of many student journalists who have learned, through trial and error, the rules of good conduct in alternative journalism.

◆ *"Bookending" the story.* The most important part of any story is its lead paragraph—the beginning sentences that either set the tone for the story by use of an anecdote or summarize what is to follow in an inviting way. A good "lead" not only encapsulates the story and answers the basics that are familiar to journalism students (who-what-when-where-how-why), but also advertises the story as worth reading.

End the story gracefully. A good way to do this is with a quote, since a writer often will wind up relying on his personal opinions if he tries to summarize the story himself. Think of the conclusions you write for term papers, and you'll realize how strong the temptation is to editorialize.

◆ *On interviews.* When conducting face-to-face interviews, avoid using a tape recorder. Even if you get permission to tape, there is something about a recording device that tends to suck the energy out of your subject. A written interview often works better because the subject feels important watching you write down his every word. The exception is in the case of verbatim interviews that you plan to run as stories in themselves. These are usually interviews of important figures who know what they're agreeing to and how to speak to a running tape recorder. You should get permission to tape at all times, especially on the telephone.

"Off the record" really isn't—if you're careful. Your subject informs you that he is about to say something off the record. The first thing you do is shut off your tape recorder and put down your pen. The next thing you do is widen your ears. "Off the record" often is a code word for "Don't attribute this to me, but I thought you should know." What you do with this information is up to your discretion. Don't write later, "A source who asked for anonymity said…" because that's not what was transacted. You can offer to cite him anonymously. If that doesn't work, instead just listen up. Afterward, try to find another authority to whom you can attribute the information. Even if you strike out, the information still serves the purpose of giving you something to file away as background material. It may even lead your research in a new direction.

◆ *On editorials.* The opinion page isn't a license for laziness. Relying solely on your argumentative powers, and maybe a few quotes from a conservative's syndicated column, will make you look like an armchair conservative. If the topic is noncontroversial, usually you can't provide enough information off the top of your head to keep the piece interesting. If it's controversial and you're not relying on good research, you're just making yourself look foolish.

◆ *On humor.* The tone of the humor is as important as the content. Sarcasm and ridicule are effective tools of the culture wars but must be used with caution lest your readers interpret them as personal attacks. You should take on the ordinary, the absurd, and the pompous. Most topics can be twisted to give everybody a good, guilt-free laugh.

## FOR EDITORS

Once a story has been handed in, it may require anything from minor changes to a complete rewrite. Because your writers are volunteers, editing is a double-edged process. You must balance your writers' egos with the need to edit stories for style and content.

The following pointers are intended to help you edit both effectively and diplomatically:

◆ Begin by scanning the whole story to get a sense of its readability. One Collegiate Network alumnus, media critic Terry Teachout, calls this a "reconnaissance mission." Judge how much work this story will need and whether you can edit the story completely in one pass, or two passes, or whether you should take one pass, circle the most glaring problems in the story, then call your writer before proceeding further. Good communication will cut down on surprises and will ease the task of pointing out major problems in the writer's submission.

◆ Edit the story with the average student in mind. As important as research and skillful argument are, the prose needs to hold the attention of your classmates. Break long sentences into two or three. Trim long quotations by using ellipses or by cutting off the speaker at a natural break and inserting a period or comma. Alternative journalism needn't read like scholarship to convey important ideas.

◆ Check facts. If a story relies heavily on new research not widely known, and the subject matter is sensitive, identify the writer's sources. If you believe more checking is needed, ask the writer—or even better, a new recruit—to do it.

◆ It's just as important to make your point as it is to be journalistically credible. Sometimes you can correct the imbalance by rewriting the lead paragraph and key transitional sentences in the articles. Other times the research will seem to plod along, giving information but lacking any bite. Was this the result of a weak story angle? Or was the angle more watered down as the story was written? In either case, your writer may have researched well, but now needs to write a more provocative story. Better to rewrite than to waste a good topic.

◆ Stick to written guidelines of style. Normally you should refer to the *Associated Press Stylebook and Libel Manual* when a question of usage arises. Sometimes, however, you will want your own standard peculiar to your school. You should have a rule for every common usage not covered by *AP*, including the rule for referring to your own publication (the most common usages are ALL CAPS and small caps). Keep an up-to-date list of these rules handy when editing.

◆ Avoid self-indulgence, that is, the use of inside jokes or unfamiliar jargon that excludes most of your readership. Delete humor that doesn't work for you or for the average reader. Replace jargon with ordinary terms.

◆ Edit the style or tone of an article with caution. If a writer has an unorthodox style, bounce the story off another editor. But apart from editing for libel, be careful you aren't simply rewriting stories, the net result being that they read as though the same person wrote them all. In general, your writers feel more appreciated when you neither under-edit nor over-edit their work.

Finally, once editing is completed, time should be reserved before the issue is sent to press so that the story may get one final proofreading by someone who is checking only spelling, grammar, and sentence structure. Many proofreaders swear by a method of "backwards reading": they start with the last paragraph and begin reading up, one paragraph at a time. That way they read complete sentences, but in no logical sequence, so they aren't distracted by content.

## THE DOUBLE STANDARD

We have discussed the need for guidelines in writing stories. These can be thought of collectively as journalistic standards. They will serve you well should you decide to go into the professional ranks. There is, however, another standard you should be aware of, if you aren't already, because it affects you directly as an alternative journalist in a hostile environment—your campus.

You and the other members of the publication's core group are a minority at the university. You know this. You also know that your views are not popular with certain administrators, faculty, and students. Some of them will react with angry letters or perhaps confront you in class or elsewhere on campus. Worse, you may get a letter from a hitherto unknown bureaucrat of the school warning you about the tone of your publication and hinting that if the tone doesn't change, the future of your paper will be brought to a vote before a new *ad hoc* Committee on Academic Diversity and Cultural Sensitivity.

It is not uncommon for conservative campus journalists to be victims of thuggery. More than one hundred cases of campus newspaper vandalism have been documented since 1993. In 1997 the *Cornell Review* was burned publicly—on two occasions—with the tacit approval of Dean of Students John Ford. In 1999, two *Duke Review* editors were physically threatened for views they expressed in letters to Duke's daily paper.

What is going on here?

You have been found guilty of violating the *double standard.* You will be judged by a different yardstick by faculty, administrators, and liberal student government types who will try to bring you to heel and influence the content of your paper rather than simply provide funding, which is their job. Your campus opponents can chant the words "diversity" and "multiculturalism," for instance, or hurl at you the tired charge of "racism." They can depend on a ready-made phony frame of reference to obscure the specifics of their position, and they can count on the support of cowardly administrators and left-wing faculty.

Double standards not only increase your responsibilities, but in the heat of the "war of ideas" they also *decrease* the responsibility your opponents feel for their own standards. Many times, these folks don't even believe in standards. Thus, your professors can advance whatever agenda they please under the guise of "Introduction to Political Theories" or "Modern Literary Criticism" or any number of other disingenuously named classes. And your administration can wreak the most partisan havoc on your campus in the name of "diversity."

But you have to play by different rules. And even if you succeed, you will never meet the expectations of some of your most vocal opponents, nor will you convert them by sticking to higher standards than they do.

Because your publication opposes the politically correct views of the radical Left, you will get no respect from the most extreme members of that clique—who unfortunately often turn out to be your professors and deans. These are the people who will harass and berate you for your mere existence. Don't worry about them. Ignore them except to hold them accountable in the pages of your paper. Their argumentative skills are probably rusty from having it their way for so long, so they may flee from the field without firing a rhetorical shot.

Each publication has its own tone. Think of the *New York Times, Time* magazine, *USA Today,* and you think of a certain tone or style unique to that publication. Your stories should indicate you will pull no punches advocating your point of view. Certainly a commitment to responsible journalism, a recruiting strategy that welcomes apolitical as well as political staffers, and a format that includes news and features as well as opinion are admirable goals insofar as they make reading your publication a respectable practice around campus. But at the same time, leave readers with the understanding that you believe some things are wrong with your school and the world beyond. Make it clear that you intend to make noise about them until they are righted.

## The Usual Suspects

As you grow to understand the structure and hierarchy of your campus, you will identify not only a well-organized student Left, but also fellow travelers in the faculty and administration. These three groups form what might be called the "iron triangle." In dealing with each of these groups, you must develop a strategy for confronting the more extreme elements in such a way that you also win over the majority who, quite likely, agree with your paper on the basics but have been cowed into silence by a shrill leftist minority. Let's consider each of these groups.

The *student Left* is the one group you are not likely to get friendly with. Most of its members are extremists and act with impunity, because they know the administration will not prosecute students who act in the name of "environmentalism," "diversity," or "multiculturalism." Some of these students even work for the establishment paper as reporters and editors, are open about their extreme political beliefs, and express them in print. Your publication, by virtue of the double standard, has no such luxury. Do not let them worry you. They take themselves too seriously and have no sense of humor. After all, they *are* out to save the world.

As for the *faculty,* while there are always a few outspoken radicals and conservatives on your campus, most of your professors are much more reserved about expressing their political views. Countless of them are so absorbed in their research or disgusted with faculty politics, or both, that they are genuinely apathetic. Most faculty are fair and appreciate students who are serious about ideas and who can argue effectively. However, since many are leftists you will have to know your subject matter better than most students.

Then there is the *administration,* which has been known to oppose an alternative publication's existence outright. At other times a school will blatantly endorse a double standard by providing funding and ideological support to activist groups and the daily paper, while ignoring those who espouse different views. Most other colleges, claiming disinterest in student affairs, won't help an embattled alternative publication. It is a sign of our troubled times that many administrators are closet conservatives or old-fashioned liberals who will privately acknowledge your right to publish and to claim recognition as an official student group, but who flinch at the prospect of defending your rights against the interests that oppose you.

The best defense against "the usual suspects" who lurk amidst these three groups is to adhere closely to the highest journalistic standards. Beyond that, here are two more suggestions:

◆ It is a good idea to leave the practice of direct political advocacy to a separate student group such as College Republicans. You should work with conservative groups on your campus in promoting speakers, arranging interviews with them, and reporting on their events *generally*. Just ensure that the political group has its own organization with its own leaders (your membership and theirs may overlap), and that your publication doesn't engage in exactly the same activities as they do.

◆ Be pragmatic in controversies. Ostensibly, you're a minority. You can't win the war of ideas in enemy territory. You can, however, win new readers and supporters for your publication—if not the ideas expressed in it. Don't lead crusades to abolish your school's new racial-sensitivity panel or to have a professor kicked out; instead, call into question the panel and document abuses by the professor. Those are the sorts of things that will make an impression on your readers. And perhaps someday, if you have enough readers and make your case convincingly, they will defeat that panel or that professor.

# Strategies & Tips for Landing News

**By Nick Felten**
Former Editor, *Duke Review*

News doesn't land in your lap—you have to make it. A student journalist should never lament that "there is nothing to write about." Most college campuses have plenty of fodder for critique. Outlined below are some tactics and techniques that will help you hone your skills as a reporter.

◆ **Keep your eyes open & listen carefully.** Potential objects of coverage express themselves through a variety of outlets. Leftists love to have meetings, wherein they'll share their views with anyone who will listen. Why not go and listen? They'll appreciate the turnout, and you might get some juicy quotes for the next issue, especially the stupid or far-out quotes that never make it into the main campus paper.

Scour course catalogs—some professors or graduate students can't refrain from introducing their political biases or low standards of scholarship into the course descriptions. Watch for catch phrases like "taught from a feminist perspective," "postmodernism," and the like. Show up for the first class or two before the drop/add period ends and obtain a copy of the syllabus. Will the class consist of legitimate study? Or will students get to watch "Seinfeld" reruns for credit? If it's the latter, you might want to question why anybody should pay $25,000 a year for this privilege when it's possible to tune in and see them for free.

A favorite of the savvy activist is the e-mail server. Thousands of activist groups have e-mail lists, and it's often possible to subscribe without having anybody know who you are, as long as you don't post. Ever wonder what leftists say when they think nobody's listening? Here's your chance to find out.

◆ **Publicly identify idiotic behavior and statements. Show mercy sparingly.** This goes hand-in-hand with listening to what your opponents are saying. Just knowing what's going on isn't enough; you have to go for the jugular. In all likelihood, the people who run the main campus newspaper will see eye-to-eye with the people they cover—the standard assortment of social justice activists, student government lackeys, and "oppressed" minority students. This stultifying arrangement produces formulaic articles of the sort where Activist Group X has a meeting or a speech, Activist Y makes a bold pronouncement, and Student Z gives the open-minded and approving "man-on-the-street" quote. This does not make for exciting journalism. Fortunately, this lack of serious debate provides your opening. Most people who make bold public pronouncements are not accustomed to having their vacuity or lack of veracity pointed out. Call them on their claims. Check their facts. Dissect their reasoning, or lack thereof. It makes for good copy, and it practically writes itself.

◆ **Repeat yourself.** Target the most egregious examples of leftism run amok on your campus. Point out the example, but don't let it go at that. Refer to it as many times as necessary to drive the point home and make it stick. As a media outlet, you have the power to transform a minor event or fact into a major embarrassment. You want to err toward overkill rather than in the opposite direction. A Marxist professor at Duke was quoted in *Commentary* as saying, among other things, that the job of a Marxist professor is "to form a Marxist intelligentsia for the struggles of the future." His quote became the subject of a feature called "MarxWatch," which has run in the *Duke Review* for more than ten years. In each feature we'd run the quote, put a slightly different twist on it, and offer to print the professor's unedited response in the pages of the *Review*. Eventually, "MarxWatch" assumed a life of its own and became a favorite feature of many readers. Overkill? Maybe, but it got the job done, as readers of the *Review* associated this professor, a department chair, with "MarxWatch."

◆ **Use propaganda effectively.** Propaganda is not a bad word— today, it's called advertising. Go ahead, promote yourself. Nobody will do it for you. Your paper won't have as much impact if the general perception is that nobody reads it. It's helpful to refer often to your "legions of readers," your "hordes of fans," the "hundreds of letters arriving daily," and all the other things one would expect of a paper that is the talk of the campus. When you take a campus figure to task, you want this person to believe his sins are being laid bare before thousands of readers. You want your readers to believe it, too. And don't forget to mention your "closet readers": these are people who won't admit they read your paper, but you know they do. Let *them* know that *you* know.

◆ **Don't apologize.** If you do your job of rattling cages on campus, a time may come when an aggrieved person or group will demand that you apologize for some perceived insult. Don't succumb. Apologizing will not make your opponents more charitably inclined toward your point of view, nor will it convince anybody that you're really okay. Indeed, it will do just the opposite. Your apology will be read by your opponents as weakness, a sign that you lack the courage of your convictions. They view it as a confession: they're right, and you're wrong. Your apology will be recycled and used against you. Left-wing zealots are good at sniffing out weakness. An apology will only bring demands for further concessions, contrition, and penance.

Not too long ago, *National Review* came under fire from the ethnic grievance industry for printing a cover deemed insensitive and offensive to Asian-Americans. Editor John O'Sullivan appeared on the "Today" show to face an indignant ethnic activist, who pressed O'Sullivan for an apology. Did he apologize? Of course not. O'Sullivan knew that the Left would simply hang that apology around his neck like a punishment stone. He turned the tables on his opponent and demanded that *she* apologize for slandering the good name of his magazine. He was unapologetic, yet retained his sense of humor. It's an example worth studying for any student who finds himself in a similar campus situation.

◆ **Be the underdog.** The local media may be *simpatico* on many issues with your school's administration, but that doesn't mean your paper won't receive favorable coverage. Since media types see themselves fighting a stuffy, conservative establishment, they look favorably upon anyone they perceive in a parallel situation. Should your school threaten you and your paper for any illegitimate reason, call the administration's bluff. If the school backs down, you win, and you've got a good story for the next issue. If the school persecutes you, send out press releases, notify alumni, and give the administration a public black eye. Emphasize the freedom of speech principle: the media will *always* side with you. The school eventually backs down, you win, and you have a great story for the next issue. In either case, a gloating editorial is *apropos*—dare them to do it again. Schools hate bad publicity; it creates work for the public relations department. More important, it can hinder fundraising. Money is the mother's milk not just of politics, but of higher education.

◆ **Inform alumni.** While we're on the topic of money: do keep in touch with your school's alumni. It is usually difficult for them to discover what's really going on at their alma mater— barring a major scandal, the only news they hear is what the public affairs and alumni departments want them to hear. An untapped market for honest reporting exists, and it's your job to fill the demand.

Obtain a copy of the alumni directory from your school. Older alumni's views tend to be more congruent with yours. They'll also have more money and thus might support your paper. You may be able to obtain a list of alumni who make annual donations; if not, perhaps a sympathetic alum who's on the alumni fundraising committee can help you.

If you do assemble a significant alumni base, make this known. Trumpet it in your own publication, and encourage the alumni to write or call your school as well. Monitor your school's response: is it honest and forthcoming? If not, point this out to the alumni and back it up with facts.

◆ **Be well read.** Your opponents won't be. Who has time to learn about Aristotle's metaphysics when there's a protest to be organized? If your paper speaks up in favor of the Western canon and Western civilization in general, then put your study time where your mouth is. You'll think, write, and argue more clearly and effectively.

◆ **Finally: be humorous.** Humor is a great way to attract readers. So loosen up—don't worry what the Left says about you. No matter *what* you do, they will oppose you. Don't strive to be thought of as "serious" and "respectable." On campus, those words equate to irrelevant and ineffective. The people who chide conservative papers for not being serious and respectable are the same people who have the most to lose by the presence of a well-written, hard-hitting, irreverent paper.

Remember, you aren't entering a popularity contest. Only sycophants start a newspaper to make friends.

# Investigative Reporting: The Basics

**By Jeff Giesea**
Former Editor, *Stanford Review*

I had a hunch that a Stanford education does little to improve its students' cultural literacy.

My skeptical side kicked in to investigate the merits of my hypothesis, and I compiled a survey of six basic questions to test students' knowledge of basic cultural facts, such as who authored *The Wealth of Nations*. With the help of the staff of the *Stanford Review*, I administered the test randomly to more than 150 Stanford upperclassmen. I discovered that after at least two years at Stanford, students still had significant gaps in their knowledge of basic cultural facts—and I had numbers to prove it.

In the resulting article, I juxtaposed the survey results with Stanford's curricular absurdities to show how the students' ongoing cultural illiteracy is tied to Stanford's devotion to academic fads at the expense of traditional education.

The article was a success. Shocked alumni called the administration; faculty advocates of traditional education used the survey results in curricular committees to push for reform; and the university PR office fretted about the possibility of the survey results appearing off-campus. Their fears were justified when *National Review* reprinted the article in their online magazine and the *Washington Times* printed an op-ed I wrote based on the article.

There's no reason why other Collegiate Network journalists cannot write equally hard-hitting investigative pieces. Here's my advice:

## Choosing a Topic

Choosing a topic is the first step in writing an investigative piece. My advice is to limit your domain of potential topics to your school. You have a competitive advantage as a student reporter on your campus. Cover your backyard, not the terrain of leading national publications. By doing so, you multiply your impact tenfold.

This is not to say that you should ignore national issues. If you discover, as the *Stanford Review* did, that your school's financial aid office systematically discriminates against nonapproved minorities, link the issue to larger debates about racial preferences—Prop 209, for example. Your coverage should be anchored to your campus, even though you may then place it in a broader context.

There are two kinds of topics for investigative pieces. The traditional Woodward-and-Bernstein kind deals with fresh news. A reporter sniffs out a "lead" and discovers previously unknown news. One time an alumni donor called to ask why we had not thanked him for the donation he had earmarked to us through the university gifts processing office. Since we had never received his money, we hypothesized that the gifts processing office somehow "overlooked" the donor's earmarking. So, we tested our conspiracy theory, discovered that the facts confirmed its truth, and reported our findings in the following issue of the paper. That article represented a classic fresh-news investigative report. Not long after we ran the story, the gifts processing office wrote us a check.

The second kind of investigative reporting is useful when there is no new news on the horizon. It involves conducting studies as if you were an anthropologist or sociologist studying the "civilization" of your school. What are the political party affiliations of professors? How many feminist studies courses are there relative to economics courses, and feminist studies majors relative to economics majors? What are the average SAT scores of students by race, gender, and legacy status—or why won't the university release that information? What is a typical "African-American Vernacular English" lecture like? Such are the types of research questions pursued in this kind of investigative reporting. Rather than exposing what is new, you shed light on what already exists. My cultural literacy article falls into this category.

## Pursuing Information

Once you have chosen a topic, gather information to test your hypothesis and see if you have a story. That means researching at the local voter registrar's office if you are writing on the political affiliations of faculty; interviewing people at the gifts processing office if you're investigating their dubious activities; or attending an "African-American Vernacular English" lecture if you are reviewing the course in your article. Since you want your article to be fact-based and bias-free, you should harvest as many facts as possible that substantiate your conclusions. In doing so, be aggressive yet polite, focused yet open to new possibilities.

Internet-based research through the web or Lexis-Nexis can facilitate investigations. With these tools you can discover interesting facts about administrators at your school, access student government documents and class syllabi, scrutinize the websites of people and campus organizations, and search for key statistics related to your article.

Once you have gathered information, compare it against your original hypothesis. What does the information suggest? Should you change your position on the matter? If so, how? Let the information you collect drive the substance of your article.

## WRITING THE ARTICLE

You now know what you want to say. But the question of how to say it remains.

First, treat the story as investigative news, not investigative opinion. Even if the article includes significant analysis, pitch it as news. Doing so will discipline your writing, lend credibility to your article, and, ultimately, increase its impact. People more readily trust investigative findings they read as news rather than those they read in an opinion piece. If the facts and quotes are substantial and compelling, readers will draw the correct conclusion from your article without your having to say it explicitly.

Second, frame your article to convince your readers that the story is important and relevant. The spin presents the chance to distinguish your article and influence the way your readers interpret the facts you submit. Suppose you write a story on exorbitant prices at university dining halls and the university's practice of requiring students to purchase meal plans. Frame your findings to discuss the monopoly-creating practices of the university and how they inflate the cost of attending your school while limiting students' freedom to choose where to eat. Thus framed, your article is much more effective than a spin that discusses the politics of world food prices.

Finally, grab readers with an eye-catching title, reel them in with an informative introduction, and sustain their attention with a well-written presentation of your findings. There's no point writing an article that does not engage the readers' attention.

Investigative reporting is incredibly worthwhile. You meet new people, learn more about your school, hone valuable skills, and make a difference. Take advantage of this opportunity. Remember: the Truth is out there.

Go get it.

# Writing an Editorial in 31 Steps

*The following list was adapted from remarks by Paul Greenberg, the Pulitzer Prize-winning editorial page editor of the* Pine Bluff (Ark.) Commercial, *who spoke to Collegiate Network editors at a CN Editors Conference in Raleigh, NC.*

1. Take a line.

2. Don't confine humor to the humorous editorials.

3. Vary style.

4. Use clear, sharp, palpable, tangible references, preferably local ones in local language. Write to the ear, not the eye. Write as you speak. Try a conversational tone.

5. Thinking about editorials is not a job; it's an avocation, hobby, obsession. Let no good idea escape you.

6. Address the reader directly; don't orate. Picture a particular person when writing.

7. Writing is rewriting.

8. Editing is often rewriting. Approach the editorial with a fresh eye and ear each time.

9. Write with feeling; edit with reason.

10. Three-quarters of the trick is to pick the right subject—one you feel strongly about, know a lot about, are interested in.

11. Put writing first—before layout, before administration, before editing the columnists or the correspondence.

12. Set aside time for writing. Keep that time free even if you just sit there and think and don't write a word.

13. Attack the strongest part of your opposition's case, not the weakest. This is a sport.

14. Never hesitate to run a correction.

15. Be tough on ideas, easy on personalities.

16. Remember that the headline is part of the editorial; write it well.

17. Don't sit down to write an editorial but to say something.

18. Arrange your schedule so that you have an opportunity to review the editorial after it is written, and to re-review it. Allow time between reviews. Time or the illusion of it is the key to good writing and editing.

19. The best writing comes from some emotional spur; the best editing from reason. First feel, then think.

20. Do not talk away editorial ideas; write them out and then evaluate them.

21. Don't treat an idea or proposal or event only within its own context, in intellectual isolation. Tie it in with some larger meaning or different perspective. Write the only editorial in the country that will appear from your particular point of view, a product of your unique experience, knowledge, wisdom, viewpoint.

22. Offer the reader some mental traction. If all you can offer the reader is pap, use a cartoon instead. Don't write on a subject for no better reason than that everybody else will.

23. Keep your favorite editorial or writer in mind when you write.

24. Aim for a masterpiece, not just another editorial.

25. Consider the completed editorial a first draft.

26. Enjoy your work.

27. If you must use a cliché, or a worn phrase, change it slightly.

28. Give local topics top priority. And write about them in a knowledgeable, local way.

29. Never fudge or cheat or lie a little; you'll be glad you didn't.

30. Pay special attention to the letters column. Run letters as soon as you can.

31. Remember that writing editorials isn't a chore; it can be art, literature, therapy. In fact, it's the grandest job in the world.

# 4. Publishing Topics

THE FIRST HALF of this chapter focuses on the design and layout of your publication. The second half takes up selected business issues you will face once you start publishing:

◆ *Desktop publishing.* How to simplify production by using e-mail. Minimum computer requirements. Suggested software.

◆ *Layout.* Organization. Artwork.

◆ *Circulation.* The before, during, and after of distributing your printed issues. Mailing to complimentary and paid subscribers.

◆ *Printing.* The essentials of going to press.

◆ *Advertising.* A word about advertiser patronage.

## Desktop Publishing

Desktop publishing—the technology to produce camera-ready typeset text from one's personal computer—has changed the landscape of independent student journalism. Back in the early 1980s, CN students would spend hundreds of dollars per issue on the services of a typesetter; they now do the job themselves. Member papers submit camera-ready products to their printers, with fewer typographical errors and a better appearance.

Most college campuses now have free personal computer labs for use by their students. Writers without computers at home or in the dorm can walk in with their handwritten texts or notes, pop in disks, and start typing.

Have your writers submit their work to you by e-mail, and ensure they keep a copy as a backup. They should send stories to you as e-mail attachments, not as e-mail text. E-mail text often loses its formatting when imported into a word-processing or desktop publishing file; reformatting is tedious and a waste of time.

Stories sent as e-mail attachments (e.g., as Microsoft Word files) are easy to import into your master publication document. They are also easy to print, which is handy because edits and proofreading should be done on paper. After edits are made on paper and entered into a revised file, the revision should be printed out for proofreading. It's much easier to spot errors on paper than on screen. Only after the proofreading corrections are made should the stories be laid out in the master publication document.

Perhaps the most surprising lesson desktop publishing teaches is that most of the effort is placing the text itself. Once you have mastered the software and know where stories will run, relatively little time is spent designing. Whoever is in charge of typesetting should ensure that the following changes are made to all story files on the master publication document:

◆ The document is set in the typeface and size for standard copy (e.g., 12- or 13-point Times Roman). The line spacing is single or "auto," and the text is properly aligned (either "justified both sides" or "left justified").

◆ The indent is set to one pica (.167 inch). Most word-processing programs set their indent tab at half an inch, which looks fine on a term paper but is too much for typeset copy.

◆ Dashes are uniform; quote marks look like 66s and 99s, not match sticks. PageMaker does these steps automatically.

◆ All underlining has been converted to italic text. Underlining looks amateurish when typeset.

◆ A proper byline has been inserted.

### Minimum Computing Requirements

Your computer should have enough storage for all of the publishing software you'll need and the large publication files you'll be accumulating. It should also have enough processing power and memory to move quickly among large applications.

Only one computer used by your organization must be equipped for desktop publishing.

Two desktop publishing applications dominate the market right now: Adobe PageMaker and Quark. PageMaker takes a freestyle approach to publishing—the user is let loose almost immediately to do as he pleases. For those who prefer a more structured and precise approach, Quark is better. These two programs will save your page setup, for future use as templates, saving you valuable time when preparing a new issue. Quark lists for more than $800, but you can find savings online, from discount software shops or mail-order firms that run advertisements in industry magazines. You can buy a new version of PageMaker for under $600.

You'll want to include illustrations in your publication—editorial cartoons, photos, artwork—and for this you will need an image editing program and access to a scanner. Adobe Photoshop rules in the image-editing category. The full retail version costs about $600, but a specially packaged academic version, available to students and educators, can be had for under $300. Less-expensive options exist, but none have anywhere near the many features of Photoshop.

## LAYOUT

Layout is more of a task of organization than of style or design. A well-organized issue will almost lay itself out. Keep two checklists: one of all stories planned for the issue and another of all advertisements scheduled to run. The story checklist, called a storyboard, should be kept from the first moment of that issue's genesis. All stories that have any likelihood of making it into the issue should be listed, and spiked only when the decision not to run them is final. Add them to the next issue's storyboard. The storyboard should also list the probable page or pages where each story will run. Thus, when you actually begin to lay out the issue, you will proceed in roughly sequential order by pages—going one page after another, just as your readers do.

### ADVERTISING LAYOUT

When beginning to lay out the issue, first place the ads. Advertising has first priority; it's crucial that you don't accidentally omit any of it.

◆ Reserve a blank square for every ad that's scheduled to run, even if the finished advertisement hasn't arrived when you begin layout.

◆ Try to leave certain pages ad-free, while concentrating ads on other pages. The front page and any other pages on which you start a new section, such as features or opinion columns, are better left free of advertising. Because the stories on these pages tend to be longer than the others in your issue, they need to be designed especially well. By leaving ads off these pages, you can design their layouts with a minimum of clutter and make better use of the artwork that accompanies the stories. Other pages, meanwhile, are better suited to "clustering" advertisements—pages with shorter articles, and "jump pages" where you continue longer articles that start on previous pages. Avoid overkill, namely, filling three-quarters of a page with small and medium-sized ads.

◆ Save small ads for last. If one story runs short on one page, while a second runs long on another, you can solve the inequity by moving a small ad on the crowded page to the less crowded one—a solution preferable to cutting paragraphs out of the long article or shrinking its artwork. When two ads or more are assigned to a page, place them from the bottom up. Ad layout mirrors story layout, which flows from the top of the page down. Try to fill the bottom row of the page before building up. If you have two quarter-page ads, for instance, place them side by side, then stack a smaller ad on top (in case you have to move it to another page at the last minute).

### DISPLAYING ARTWORK

Like any publication seeking a large audience, yours should provoke the eyes. It shouldn't look difficult to read, like a textbook. Its stories should advertise themselves to the reader as he scans your pages. Artwork advertises stories.

Artwork is any drawing or original photograph that calls a reader's attention to a story. Plan artwork well in advance of your deadlines. For instance, get in the habit of assigning artwork for all your front-page stories one week before the stories are due so you and your artist can create something.

What kind of artwork is best? The kind you create yourself (as opposed to reprinting from another source). And the kind you can generate with the least difficulty and the most creativity. For these reasons, an eager friend with a camera is a necessity. Give him a roll of film for every issue and say to him, "Go!" A camera is a good investment for your publication. If you run an exposé of the administration, you should go beyond naming names. Include photographs.

Ask interview subjects for informal photographs instead of studio poses. When you run artwork, *always run it large.*

As for where your artwork should run in relation to the story, just remember it's there to advertise. Don't relegate your artwork to the margins of pages. It should showcase the story with its size and strategic placement.

### THREE LAYOUT TOOLS

Three tools of production craftsmanship will add professional touches to every page you design:

◆ *White Space.* White space is that pica (.167 inch) or two that separates the edges of a column of text from the advertisement or border tape running parallel to it; it is that buffer between a headline and the accompanying story; it is any place within the margins of your page without text or artwork on it. White space is similar to artwork in the task it performs, though it is more subtle. It provides graphical relief and makes the text in its immediate vicinity appear less intimidating. You should allow white space in many places throughout your issue. It is one of the true secrets of professional layout design.

Pick up copies of professional newspapers you consider smart-looking, and see how they do it. The big chains—Knight-Ridder, Gannett, Times Mirror—show what you can accomplish with a little white. One way to increase white space to let your stories breathe is to left justify all text. This is called "right ragged." Try it and see what effects it produces.

◆ *Borders.* Borders are used to separate stories, add graphical relief to a page design, or "box in" a special item. (On desktop publishing programs they are often called "stroke.")

The first rule of bordering is to use hairline borders abundantly. If two stories run side by side, use hairline in the center of the "gutter" (the white space that separates the stories) to divide them. If you publish a magazine, use hairline to divide every column on every page, or just on sidebars to distinguish them from the accompanying stories. Use hairline to separate ads from copy. Hairline should be the only border you use to make vertical lines (all the others are too thick). Besides hairline, try to stick to only two or three line sizes. Many papers use hairline and either 2- or 4-point exclusively. One-point works better than hairline when surrounding a photo because it has better definition.

Be sure there's always at least a full pica (.167 inch) between the text and border on each side. If you don't have room for at least a pica, make room. You *need* that white space.

◆ *Knowledge.* You will acquire other knacks of successful layout as time goes on. These include writing headlines, arranging text and graphics for maximum effect, and of course making the whole process more efficient. There is also a knack to working with the camera room at your printer. Unless you are sure that a drawing or reprinted artwork is camera-ready, have the printer shoot a halftone of it and place it in the designated area. Ask somebody in the camera room how this is done.

As you improve your skills you will find it important to put the knowledge you obtain into writing. Just as you need a reliable writing style manual, such as the *AP Stylebook*, to give you consistent guidelines for copyediting, so you need a style manual for layout. In other words, right from your first issue, you must set standards and stick to them. One easy way to do this is to read over each new issue carefully, marking errors in your layout or designs, then decide how you will improve them.

Your familiarity with your desktop publishing software will also increase with every issue. While you don't want to use every bell and whistle that PageMaker has to offer, you do want to become familiar with features like "text wrap," "grouping," and others that will decrease the amount of time you spend in the layout process. One tip: be sure to set up a template for your publication, so that you will not have to retype the page headers and masthead for every single issue. The Collegiate Network recommends books like *PageMaker for Dummies*, which highlights the most useful features about the software package. While it takes diligence to learn these skills, it's worth your time in saved hours.

## LAST THINGS

Before submitting your work to the printer, you naturally want to confirm, to the best of your ability, that all work was done properly.

Do two things: First, ensure that all advertising runs as planned. Second, have somebody on hand late in the production session who has not been working on the boards. This person should carefully read over every page and check for production errors. It will surprise you how many mistakes a pair of fresh eyes can catch.

You are now ready for the printer. Be sure you have indicated every place where artwork or color processing will be done by the camera room, and put all artwork in a separate envelope in the shipping container so it isn't lost or damaged. Enclose a sheet that lists the pressrun and color you want (even if you have already discussed this with the printer) and any special instructions.

## CIRCULATION

Distributing your paper is perhaps the least glamorous job connected with student journalism, but it is as important as any other—without it, no one reads your paper.

Distribution responsibility is an excellent way for freshmen to prove themselves. You want young people who have the dedication and drive to do the small, mundane things that will help your paper succeed. More often than not, it is the people who distribute the paper who contribute the most. In fact, it is in the ranks of faithful and reliable distributors that you could find your next publisher. Regardless of who distributes the paper, it *must* be distributed, even if you—the editor—do it yourself.

How you distribute your paper is as important as who distributes it. After working countless hours on a first-class product, don't make the mistake of plunking down four stacks of 1,000 papers in the student union and expect more than a handful of people to read it. Use imagination and lots of common sense when distributing:

◆ Don't distribute the entire pressrun on one day in a few well-traveled spots.

◆ Instead, scatter distribution over an entire week—for example, on Monday, Wednesday, and Friday—hitting at least ten distribution sites on each day.

◆ Never distribute your paper in piles of more than one hundred; it's too easy for intolerant leftists to dump them. The theft and burning of conservative student newspapers is becoming common on college campuses. If you're going to get around these obstacles, smart distribution is essential.

Distributing your publication requires planning and follow-up. Think of circulation as having three distinct stages instead of one, and you'll be able to do it more effectively.

### Before Distribution Day

Plan to publish on a certain day of the week or month and stick to that day all year. For one thing, your printer may not be able to accommodate you if you keep shifting the day of publication. Second, it assists your ad salespeople in dealing with clients if they can guarantee publication on a certain day of the week. Third, it gets students in the habit of looking for your publication on a certain day. That habit is reinforced if you come out on Monday or Friday, because these days stick in the mind as the beginning and end of the week.

### On Distribution Day

The best place for you to circulate your issues is twelve to eighteen inches from your rival publication. Students are creatures of habit. They look for the student daily in the same place each day. *That's* where you should distribute your paper— alongside the daily and in other places on campus where students habitually pick up freebies. Think about it. Every day of

the week you know where you are likely to be when you see
the first stack of today's dailies. Monday, Wednesday, and Friday,
for instance, you may be coming out of your 10 a.m. class,
while on the other two days you spot the issues at your dorm
just before lunch. Even if you don't actually pick up your competition every day, the point is that you are in the habit of seeing
it at a certain place. That is the kind of habit you want to instill
in your readers—and what better way than to build off their
existing habit for your competition? Here are some things to
keep in mind on distribution day:

◆ Whoever picks up the issues at the printer should remember
to retrieve the production boards that you sent there. Printers
often get busy, forget about your boards, and lose them—and
with them the originals of advertisements or artwork that you
had planned to reuse!

◆ Count the number of issues wrapped into a bundle. This will
expedite your dropoffs because you'll be able to think in terms
of bundles (i.e., if you count 200 issues per bundle, then a
dropoff of 400 is two bundles, 100 is half a bundle, and so on).

◆ Prepare a list of all dropoff sites and the number of copies to
drop at each. The site descriptions should be as exact as possible (e.g., main library plaza entrance: 200 copies). The list
should be compiled in sequential order, beginning with classrooms, where copies will go quickly if you drop them off before
classes start. Locations like the student union and the library,
where your stacks erode only gradually during the day, should
be last.

◆ When delivering, the driver should know where the establishment paper gets dropped off at each site on the list, and aim for
the same location. The university will probably let you drive on
campus sidewalks in the early morning, but ask permission first.
If the daily uses circulation boxes, avoid using them (unless you
have permission). Instead, drop off your issues right next to
theirs.

Several of your staff should be familiar with the circulation
route so that you can visit the sites during the day and see how
things are going. For instance, if you are walking to class and

notice all the papers gone at a prominent dropoff site, one of three things has happened: all the papers have been picked up and presumably are in the hands of nearby students; the driver is late; or the papers have been stolen. If you suspect theft, check nearby garbage cans. It's hard to carry a bundle of loose newspapers very far. You can save many papers this way.

### AFTER DISTRIBUTION

From your observations during the day, make adjustments to your distribution list where you feel it's appropriate. If large stacks were left over at several spots, you may be circulating too many copies. Cut your pressrun. Or maybe they simply need to be redistributed. Also, save a few bundles and circulate them at a timely opportunity between issues. For instance, you could leave a fresh bundle every Friday in the student union and in the library. These locations will attract readers from off campus as well as students who missed you the first time around.

### SUBSCRIPTIONS, FREE AND PAID

For your paper to have lasting impact, you must connect with alumni. They can support you financially and morally, so never miss a chance to put your newspaper in their hands. The ideal time for this is at your weekly football game, especially on homecoming. Scatter your staff at several entrances to the stadium and pass out your paper by hand. Alumni will *always* take your paper. They *love* students and any publication that can tell them what really goes on at their alma mater. This is a great way to pick up subscribers and to circumvent the monopoly on information held by your school's information office.

◆ Prominent media contacts are interested in your publication: John Leo, columnist at *U.S. News & World Report;* R. Emmett Tyrrell Jr., editor of the *American Spectator;* Richard Lowry, editor of *National Review;* John Fund, an editor of the *Wall Street Journal's* editorial page; and David Horowitz of *Heterodoxy.* All of these men follow the independent student newspaper movement and would appreciate copies of your publication. Also send it to media celebrities such as Nat Hentoff of the liberal *Village Voice* if you're feeling confident. Hentoff came out swinging against the Cornell University administration on more than one occasion when the *Cornell Review* was stolen and burned in 1997.

◆ Observers from the community are also interested. They include the local media (including community weeklies), elected officials, like-minded political or cultural organizations, think tanks, and the like. You never know when a journalist, politician, or sympathetic person unknown to you will pick up your issue and read it.

Sell subscriptions right away. In every issue, simply reserve a quarter-page or so for a subscription ad that includes a cut-out coupon to mail in. You should charge at least $25 for a one-year subscription, because those who pay it will realize that it is a gift to your new enterprise.

If you want to capitalize on the entering freshman class, you should send a mailing to all freshman parents with a prepared subscription form and reply envelope. Labels can be obtained from the registrar's office. Most special interest and minority groups are allowed these lists, so there is no reason why the same standard shouldn't also apply to you. Parents of new students are excellent targets because many of them are interested in what goes on at this school to which they have just sent a loved one and a large check. You may want to charge a discounted "parents' rate."

The *Red and Blue* at Penn carried this out in 1996, netted more than $4,000, and broke the school's monopoly on information that goes to freshman parents. Once parents subscribe, chances are they will renew the following year. Mailing an issue to freshmen is also a way to attract incoming students and give them a taste of the school's conservative spirit.

## PRINTING

Effective publishing involves balancing quality and quantity. Several variables affect that balance: frequency of publication, number of pages per issue, staff, and financial resources. A word now about circulation—the number of copies you want to print and distribute.

◆ Suppose you want to publish a political monthly. You are at a state school where the establishment daily circulates 25,000 copies. Assume you have deep pockets and can afford an identical pressrun of 25,000. Are you sure you can circulate all those copies? Or will thousands be left in their stacks around campus, embarrassing you and cheering your rivals? It might be wiser to choose a smaller circulation, of around 10,000. With the money you were going to spend on 15,000 extra issues, you could print four more pages per issue, or ten issues this year instead of eight.

◆ On the other hand, suppose you attend a private college where the daily paper circulates 7,500 copies. You would like to publish on high-quality paper, but you know this will increase your per-issue costs. The printers have said that the kind of product you want to publish will cost roughly $1,000 per issue for 2,500 copies, and $1,800 for 5,000 copies. At this rate, you determine you should be able to publish six times this year. But were you to publish on inexpensive paper, you could not only publish more frequently, but could probably afford a pressrun equivalent to the daily's—a manageable number to circulate at 7,500. And with desktop publishing, there is no reason why your cheap issue couldn't look almost as attractive as an expensive one.

As the above scenarios demonstrate, your circulation (also known as your pressrun size) affects all the other variables involved in making a printing decision. The higher the circulation, the higher your publication's visibility. If people are seen reading your issues all over campus—in the classroom buildings, the lunch halls, and the dorms—it can't be ignored. And increasing your circulation involves relatively low risk. Most of what a printer charges you is for production of the mechanical plates that are used on the presses. Spinning the presses for a few extra minutes is cheap by comparison. So although a pressrun of 5,000 may cost $700, another 1,000 copies may cost only an extra $50. Boosting your circulation can be a very cost-effective way to increase impact.

### CHOOSING A PRINTER

One of your earliest and most important decisions is choosing a printer. Prices vary widely; your mission is to find the cheapest one around. If a printer eighty miles away gives you a much better price than any in town, then spend the extra gas money and take your business to him.

Before shopping for a printer, make a checklist of the items you will need to give each printer for estimating purposes.

◆ *Number of copies.* Shoot for a pressrun of your school's enrollment, or 50 percent of enrollment if it's more than 8,000. Ask the printer about the price of extra or fewer copies, in round numbers (per 1,000). The first copies that roll off the presses always cost the most because the issue's start-up costs are included.

◆ *Type of paper.* Unless you are starting on more than a shoe-string, you should print on the least expensive paper available: thirty-seven-pound newsprint. And not the kind that is pre-cut into letter-sized sheets, but the big rolls that are cut and folded right on the presses. Usually only a few presses in any given market accommodate all the people publishing at high volumes on newsprint. So if your community has an inexpensive-looking weekly newspaper, find out where it is printed. Find out also who prints the establishment paper and inquire with the city newspaper. These should be the first printers you visit because chances are they are the best deals in town. To be sure, however, use your telephone and the Yellow Pages to identify all the other offset web presses within about fifty miles.

◆ *Format.* Some offset web presses are configured for only one type of format. So even if a printer has the equipment you need, he may be unable to do your magazine with a staple in the middle because all his clients are tabloid-sized, double-fold, loose-leaf newspapers.

◆ *Number of pages.* When you find a compatible printer, tell him to quote a price for a twelve-page issue if you've decided on a tabloid newspaper, twenty-four pages if a magazine. These sizes will give your publication a good thickness.

◆ *Spot color.* It should not cost more than $200 per issue to use a single primary color to highlight items on the four pages that make up that mechanical plate. If you pay to use green on the front page of a twelve-page issue, for instance, you can also use green on pages 6, 7 and 12. Often this is known as your second color on the plate, the first color being black. For now, answer "yes" to this question.

*Printers will ask about the information discussed above. Know it when you approach them.* Also be aware that compared with your printer's major accounts, your publication, even at a circulation of 10,000 or 15,000, is a minor job. Where larger papers will take hours on the pressrun floor, yours will be coughed out in twenty minutes or so. High-volume accounts make it possible for publications like yours to print cheaply, but their schedules may conflict with yours.

Find out what days of the week are best for the printer to squeeze you in. Later, when you decide on the day you want to publish, you may find one printer more convenient to use than another that is similarly priced.

Exactly what combination of pressrun and page length you use, and how many issues you publish this year, will be fine-tuned once you start publishing and circulating issues. Plan on a higher-than-usual pressrun for your debut issue. For now, at least you have the figures that will enable you to determine your per-issue cost. And that will be 85 percent of your first-year budget.

## Working with Printers

One of your most important business relationships is with your printer. It is a relationship in which you make certain demands. One demand involves circulation. For instance, if you plan to drop issues primarily at dorm cafeterias and the student union, you can't wait till noon to get them printed. If you target classroom buildings and dormitories early in the day, when students are heading to classes, print your job at the crack of dawn. If after the first couple of issues it becomes apparent that the printer cannot ensure that this happens consistently, you must rework your own production schedule or find another printer.

Another demand is that the quality of the printed product be acceptable. For this the camera room is primarily responsible. The pressroom's only task is to deliver your pressrun in copies that don't look splotchy or faint. The guys in the camera room control everything else: they "shoot" your artwork on the pages in a process known as halftoning, and it is required of most photographs and other complex art.

After the first issue, visit the person in charge of the camera room. Ask him to suggest ways you can make his work easier. Study your printing bill. If there are numerous camera room charges that don't make sense to you, ask him about these. He may tell you how to eliminate unnecessary work that your production technique has forced him to charge you for. If you cannot get a consistently good product out of the camera room, or the personnel seem uncooperative, switch printers.

Finally, your printer is the most important business account your publication will have. Always be on excellent financial and communicative terms with the printer. Always notify the printer in advance of any special issues or printing jobs you need done.

◆ Be sure that you and anyone else who plays a significant role on the publication have your own telephones with voice-mail and that you check e-mail. E-mail is a must; most days it will be the only way you can communicate with your colleagues.

◆ Before your first issue comes out, get a bulk-rate mailing permit from your local U.S. Postal Service branch. It's inexpensive and requires little paperwork. It is an all-purpose tool for mailing your product, as well as literature such as advertising promotions, en masse. There are actually two types of bulk-rate permits: regular and nonprofit. The post office has its own method of verifying your not-for-profit status: you submit two items that are reviewed by a postal employee, who decides if your literature is nonprofit. If for some reason you are denied a nonprofit permit, don't worry. Regular bulk-rate stamps don't cost that much more and are still far cheaper than first-class mail. Besides, you can always apply again.

## Advertising

Now, to accounts receivable, which leads inevitably to a discussion of selling advertising. To make money selling ads you need four things: a pricing strategy, a rate card, salespeople, and a good billing system.

### Pricing

An alternative publication has two pricing structures: what you *say* you charge and what you actually charge. The formal prices are listed in the rate card, while the informal prices are negotiated by your salespeople as they try to convince merchants to advertise. The formal structure is important because it gives the price ceiling—the maximum amount you will ever make from one ad. If your price ceiling is too high, your salespeople may be turned away immediately, without getting a chance to negotiate a lower price. If it's too low, you might lose hundreds of dollars a year in extra revenue that advertisers would be willing to pay.

◆ Charge less than your competition does. If your publication and theirs are in the same format (such as tabloid), you can list your prices at a certain fraction of your competitor's—for example 70 percent. Better to charge less money if it helps your people sell ads while they learn the knack of negotiating.

◆ Look for selling advantages and play them up. Your salespeople could benefit by having a sheet they could include with the advertising rate card (discussed below), demonstrating how your publication's advertising prices beat the competition's. A prime example is *discounts.* Every publication offers volume and frequency discounts to advertisers. Make sure your discounts are better than everybody else's.

◆ Another selling advantage is *the price-per-reader cost.* Suppose the campus daily charges $800 for a full-page ad, and circulates 16,000 copies. Its price per reader will be 5.0 cents per page. Now let's suppose there is a literary magazine on campus that circulates 4,000 copies, and its rate per reader is 4.0 cents ($100 per page). If your publication is circulating 10,000 copies, a good strategy would be to charge $250 per page, thus offering wider visibility than the other magazine, better value than the daily, and a price-per-reader cost that is unmatched by either. Show off the advantage.

◆ Make the most of the comparison between your publication and your competition. For instance, if you are a magazine competing with a tabloid, you should charge for a full page no more than what your competition charges for a half. Then your salesperson can hold up identically priced examples of each— your full page ad, their smaller one (be sure to choose one from a particularly cluttered ad page)—and tout your publication's "Ad Placement Advantage" to the prospective advertiser.

◆ Don't get bogged down in column inches. Comparing two products should be as easy as showing an unattractive sample of theirs and an attractive sample of yours. If the advertiser still has doubts, it's time to enhance the comparison by offering a discount.

◆ Structure your rates to encourage advertisers to buy larger ads. Perhaps charge $250 for the full page, $150 for the half, and $80 for the quarter.

### THE RATE CARD

A rate card is the right arm of any salesperson. It not only states the prices, but it also lists all the advertising policies of your publication. If done properly, the rate card provides instant credentials to a merchant whom you approach for a sale and answers his questions. An ad contract and a smartly done rate card are the only two things your salespeople need to take to a prospective advertiser.

You can publish the rate card using your computer. Afterward, take it to the printer and spend a few extra dollars to have copies made on high-quality, sturdy paper with spot color. A good rate card lists all prices, discounts, and policies; shows diagrams of the popular ad sizes in proportion to the page size; includes information about your school's student market; and (very important) gives your circulation figure. The newspaper's philosophy shouldn't be included unless you can turn it into a selling point. The actual text in your rate card should be minimal and restricted to selling points.

## AD STAFF

Sales is a tough line of work. To succeed in it you need to be pragmatic and relentless in the face of frustration. The people who sell ads for your publication will have to be inspired to press on after their last five contacts have said "no." Generally this inspiration comes in the form of cash incentives—commissions paid on each ad sold. Since your publication is small and the flow of cash will not be substantial at first, those commissions will have to be a good chunk of your total sales. Twenty percent is a reasonable commission rate for you to pay salespeople.

You should put effort into recruiting your first ad salesperson, because he likely will become your first ad manager. Perhaps you will pay him a 25 percent commission, plus 5 percent of all sales made by salespeople he recruits, perhaps even 50 percent of all sales over a certain quota set by the publisher every issue. In exchange, the manager agrees to handle the paperwork (see below), train new recruits and keep track of their sales, and take care of delinquent or otherwise difficult accounts. If there is a business school on or near campus, you could post flyers advertising the position; see if the B-school has its own publication as well where you can run a classified ad.

## KEEPING TABS

For your advertising contract, use a no-carbon-required form so that you have a copy to give the advertiser at the point of sale (give him the copy and keep the original). Your contract should contain the paper's advertising policies, which should also be published on the rate card; the exact terms of the contract, including a comments space in case the salesperson needs to "customize" the sale (i.e., wheel and deal); and signature lines for the advertiser, the salesman, and either the ad manager or the publisher.

Bill your advertisers using generic no-carbon invoices rather than monthly statements so that you can collect immediately. (Send the original, keep the copy.) An invoice should list the issue in which the ad appeared, its size and cost, date of billing, and terms of payment (usually due upon receipt). If the advertiser does not pay the invoice within a couple of weeks, send a statement that lists the invoice number, date of original billing, and a statement that payment is due within ten days. Each of these should also be printed on duplicate forms; keep the copy for your records. If you must send a third billing notice, enclose a nice letter from the publisher informing the merchant that your small publication literally depends upon the prompt payment of its advertisers to stay in business and would the merchant kindly please send payment today ("thank you again for your generous patronage").

Keep bookkeeping simple, noting only the date of insertion of the ad, its cost, and payment received. Do not send statements acknowledging payment from the advertiser.

What if an advertiser doesn't pay? First, send the salesman who sold the ad to talk with the advertiser in person and by appointment if possible. Have him find out if the advertiser was unhappy with the ad in any way, and if so, offer to run it again for free. Otherwise, simply tell the advertiser the bill must be paid. If the advertiser still won't pay, at least now you know it was not just an oversight. This piece of information will come in handy when you contact the area Chamber of Commerce or Better Business Bureau.

## PATRONAGE

All staff, especially editors, should recognize that it is vital to patronize those merchants who advertise in their publication. This strategy pays immediate benefits surprisingly often. If the advertiser has run a coupon with his ad, he will notice when coupons start arriving. Likewise, if more of his students mention something advertised in his ad, he is bound to feel better about having advertised.

Encourage your staff to patronize your advertisers. They should avoid going to their competitors who don't advertise with you. A patronage strategy contributes to your overall spirit as a publication that has an outlook and a purpose, even toward its advertisers. And you should try to have your social events revolve around your advertisers' establishments as much as possible—at least the eating and drinking establishments.

## NEWSPAPER DESIGNS: PAGE ONE

Unlike magazines, a newspaper can comfortably include more than one story on its front page, with room to spare for promoting inside-page stories. Many papers follow the *Dartmouth Review's* classic design, which promotes one lead story on the front page. Others, like the *Austin Review,* use the more traditional newspaper design, which allows for several articles on the front page, usually "jumped" to the interior pages of the paper. In general, the typical newspaper format is more difficult to do well. The page can look confusing, with articles running together and headlines poorly differentiated.

The main goal of the front page is to attract readers. This is why large headlines, above the fold, with captivating pictures are so important. Collegiate Network papers are not the *New York Times,* so people do not seek out your paper for that reason. *You must give them a reason to pick it up.*

Most CN papers that use newspaper layout, print in the tabloid format. The most common page dimension for tabloids is 11x17 inches. There are other sizes as well. Inquire about them at your printer. Below are the front pages of *Contumacy* and the *Cornell Review.* Your paper may want to emulate aspects of their design.

## NEWSPAPER DESIGNS: INSIDE PAGES

The need for section headings becomes evident once you begin to organize all the stories that *don't* begin on page one. If you don't have sections, the task of placing stories in the paper becomes more difficult. Sections also give your paper *focus*. Oftentimes, people contribute stories that are merely tangential to the mission of your paper. Having section headings helps organize these pieces.

Another type of inside page that is difficult to do well is the "jump." In newspaper lingo, "jumps" are the pages that you set aside to continue the articles from the front page. Don't let these pages be mere afterthoughts. You should: (1) keep your jump pages to one story per page, whenever possible; (2) use a complete headline that runs across the entire jump; and (3) load up the remainder of the page with advertisements. The examples below demonstrate effective layout. The *Austin Review* effectively uses section headings to divide the various types of articles in the paper. The *Yale Free Press* has mastered the art of the jump, making the page look attractive with pull quotes and graphics to keep the reader interested.

**Austin Review**
**University of Texas**

**Yale Free Press**
**Yale University**

## MAGAZINE DESIGNS: COVERS

Magazine covers should attract readers. This is why it is important to have a cover that is laid out well, with large headlines and eye-catching graphics or photographs. Some papers steer toward controversy to attract readers, while some magazines are more subtle. The following examples from two of the best Collegiate Network newspapers demonstrate the design principles that produce eye-catching and stylish magazine covers. Over the years, Yale's *Light & Truth* has been famous for its cover designs, which often incorporate catchy, satirical headlines with colorful cartoons.

**Light & Truth**
**Yale University**

The *Virginia Advocate* takes a sober, professional approach, displaying photographs or artwork to attract readers to the main cover story. This does not mean that the *Advocate* steers clear of controversy. In fact, the cover below shows how the elements— large photos, balanced page design, and white space—can combine to produce a hard-hitting and visually compelling cover.

The Virginia Advocate
University of Virginia

## MAGAZINE DESIGNS: TABLE OF CONTENTS

Inside page designs are not as important for magazines as they are for newspapers, as typically the inside pages have one article per page. If you choose the magazine format for your publication you should be more concerned with the table of contents page and the cover. An effective contents page will interest readers in your magazine, whereas a poorly designed one will lead the magazine into the trash. The illustration below shows that the *Primary Source* at Tufts University has an effective table of contents page, organizing articles into departments and features. It is also attractive and professional-looking.

**The Primary Source
Tufts University**

## LAYOUT: WHAT TO DO AND WHAT NOT TO DO

Ever wonder why your paper doesn't appear as professional as you believe it should? Perhaps the problem is your approach to layout.

The most important part of your paper is not article content…it's article packaging. It doesn't matter how good your articles are if no one picks up your paper or if you have designed a reader-unfriendly paper.

Following is a guide to layout compiled by the CN over years of observation.

### Do

1) Cut articles to make room for pictures and other illustrations. Photos should *not* be reduced to make room for articles. Photos, if good, are more important than any two or three paragraphs in the article. You diminish photo impact when you reduce them to, for example, 2x3-inch size.

2) Leave white space on the page through frequent paragraphing, use of pull quotes, and wide alleys between columns. Break up the boredom of text by selecting hot or interesting quotes from the story, boldfacing them, enlarging them, and inserting them in the body. The point, of course, is to "pull" the reader into the story and to break up the gray wall of text that can look so daunting. Use the "left justification" feature to achieve the "right ragged" effect.

3) Blow photos up. No photo can be too large. Photos, particularly action photos of demonstrations and the like, invest your paper with more impact than any other single factor. When a student or administrator opens your paper to see his picture, it ought to jump off the page at him. This point cannot be overemphasized.

CN staff have seen too many fine newspaper photographs stripped of impact by reduction. Many times, the subjects in the photo are unrecognizable because of the reduction. Why bother to print a photo if you render it useless? Maximum size…maximum impact.

## Don't

1) Don't use every PageMaker feature on every page of your paper. That's not creative...that's just bad layout. Wacky fonts, cute wraparounds, and oddly cropped photos may be fun to use, but they combine to produce amateurish pages that are difficult to read and that destroy credibility. Stick with a traditional font, like Times Roman or Palatino, and stay away from cursive or wing-dings. A newspaper font should have feet. Sans serif fonts are not acceptable for newspaper text.

2) Don't fill every square inch of each page with text. Let your pages breathe with white space, photos, graphics, and the right-ragged effect.

3) Don't use a border for ads or boxes larger than 2-point for one-line boxes and 3-point for two-line boxes. Anything larger shouts "Amateur!"

4) Don't use tiny fonts like 9- or 10-point. They're almost unreadable. No one likes to squint, and people will most likely throw your paper away in disgust rather than read it. Use at least 12-point.

5) Don't use two-column layout in a tabloid-sized paper. This produces large blocks of gray text that you may find fascinating but that readers will quickly pass over.

You can have the most well-written and well-edited paper at your school, but if the layout is amateurish, cramped, self-indulgent, or otherwise unprofessional and unattractive, few people will ever read it.

# 5. Second Steps

YOU'VE LAID THE GROUNDWORK for your publication and have published an issue. You are the king of your own sovereignty. Like any good sovereign, you need to build an army, find powerful allies (if you are a wise king), assemble a cabinet, and conquer. This chapter explains how you can achieve your goals sooner rather than later in your first year of publication:

◆ *Joining the Collegiate Network.* Overview of CN programs.

◆ *Involving your alumni.* Fundraising; direct mailing versus personal visitation. How to conduct a fundraising campaign. Keeping good relations with your donors.

◆ *Preparing for year two.* Three tools to help ensure smooth transition to a new publishing year.

◆ *Handling controversy.*

◆ *Taking center stage.* One step further—holding an event.

◆ *Going digital.* Building a website for your publication.

## Joining the Collegiate Network

Admission to the Collegiate Network brings substantial benefits, and membership must be earned.

CN programs offer aspiring student writers and thinkers many opportunities for intellectual and professional growth. Your publication's editor should maintain regular contact with the Collegiate Network. The fact that you are reading this handbook indicates that you have already made contact with us. Even if your publication is not yet a member, you should not hesitate to contact the Network by telephone (800-225-2862), by mail, or by e-mail (cn@isi.org) with any questions not covered by this handbook. The CN web address—*www.collegiate-network.org*—is linked to the Intercollegiate Studies Institute (ISI) website, so you can take advantage of all the academic resources ISI has to offer.

Anyone who has a question about CN programs or about something they read in *Newslink,* the CN monthly newsletter, is encouraged to call or write. *Newslink* is a good source of information for everyone on your staff. Each CN student receives it, and we send multiple copies to all member publications, so be sure everyone in leadership gets one. Keep a couple in the office as well.

During the school year, member papers are required to send five copies of each issue to the CN as soon as the papers roll off the presses. Press clippings about your publication should be photocopied and mailed to the office. The Collegiate Network office is your advocate as well as your financial support. This is your Network, at your disposal, so use it. CN activities cover the entire year, and we encourage you to participate in them to the fullest.

### How It All Started

In 1979, two students at the University of Chicago asked a think tank for help to counter the one-sided reporting that dominated the principal student publication on their campus. Tod Lindberg and John Podhoretz, freshmen at the time, founded a newspaper that presented alternative views and received a grant to defray publishing costs. Although nobody realized it at the time, this was the start of a grassroots movement that has since grown into the Collegiate Network. This movement seeks to call higher education back to its touchstones of academic freedom, intellectual integrity, unfettered debate on social and cultural issues, and an understanding of the values of Western civilization. Lindberg is now the editor of the Heritage Foundation's *Policy Review* and Podhoretz is a columnist for the *New York Post.*

Today, this association of more than seventy independent publications operates at the nation's foremost colleges and universities. Largely free from reliance on student government approval and unconstrained by faculty "oversight boards," they are often the only truly independent student voices on campus.

During the past dozen years this influential group of Collegiate Network publications has been the most consistent and enduring opponent of the political orthodoxy that has become known as "political correctness." In so doing, these newspapers have chronicled the many startling changes taking place in the academy. Under the tutelage of the Intercollegiate Studies Institute, which administers the CN, hundreds of young editors and writers have received the intellectual training and arguments essential to making the case for liberty both in the classroom and on the pages of CN newspapers.

By documenting questionable uses of mandatory student fees, the proliferation of politicized academic departments on campus, and the stifling of debate through constitutionally dubious speech codes, the student reporters and editors of the Collegiate Network have helped set the terms of debate surrounding modern higher education.

Graduates of Collegiate Network newspapers have become professional journalists and authors in every region of the country. From the *Wall Street Journal* to *Commentary*, the *Detroit News* to the *Washington Times, Investor's Business Daily* to *National Review*, CN alums have proven themselves to be some of the brightest and most promising members of the rising generation.

The Collegiate Network is committed to helping its student publications overcome substantial obstacles, including vandalism and theft, as they present independent, alternative views on campus issues. The CN places the highest premium on excellence and accuracy. To achieve this goal, the CN has developed the range of services outlined here.

## COLLEGIATE NETWORK SERVICES

The toll-free hotline has become the Collegiate Network's most popular service. If a student needs writing, editing, or business advice, or has encountered a problem that is too big to handle alone, help is available at 800-225-2862. With the CN hotline, a friendly, experienced voice is never more than a phone call away.

*Newslink,* the newsletter of the Collegiate Network, is published quarterly. It features original articles about educational topics, as well as story ideas and practical tips for running an alternative publication. *Newslink* notifies CN papers of grant deadlines, conference schedules, internships, and job opportunities for CN members. For many papers that are not self-sufficient, the CN offers partial financial support by providing operating grants to its members. These grants, intended to defray printing costs, are awarded annually in the summer. Annual Incentives to Excellence Awards enable publications to undertake special projects not funded by normal operating grants. These competitive grants of up to $1,000 go to publications with a track record of improvement, campus focus, contact with the CN, and investigative reporting.

Editors training conferences are held on the East and West Coasts. These conferences provide practical instruction on writing, editing, recruiting, and journal design. In addition to the CN staff, conference faculty often include well-known journalists such as *U.S. News and World Report* columnist John Leo, *Village Voice* columnist Nat Hentoff, *Wall Street Journal* editorial writer John Fund, *Forbes* editor Tim Ferguson, author and former New Left activist David Horowitz, *Commentary* publisher and CN alumnus Jonathan Cohen, and author Richard Steinberg. CN alumni such as the *Charlotte Observer's* Tony Mecia and the *Public Interest's* Eric Cohen, who are now professional journalists, often address the students. The conferences provide a great opportunity for student journalists to share experiences and ideas with one another.

Since not all staff members from each paper can come to the regional conferences, the CN sends Collegiate Network program officers to visit CN publications on campus for campus training sessions. During these visits, the program officer answers questions about the Collegiate Network and provides guidance on recruiting, layout, writing, and staff structure. All CN program officers have had extensive experience with alternative journalism and will often act as a "troubleshooter" for the papers visited.

The CN sponsors internships at national publications for editors and reporters of CN member papers. Some of the positions are summer-long internships for underclassmen who will be returning to their respective schools. Other internships are for an entire year for recent CN graduates. Many graduates have already learned that running a Collegiate Network paper is much more than just another extracurricular activity—it is often the first step toward a successful career. CN graduates gain experience that, when considered with their academic degree, gives them a distinct advantage in the competitive world of professional journalism.

The CN website reaches a wide audience through the internet. It offers information about the Network's mission, provides a list of CN member publications, and offers links to CN member sites. Visit the CN at www.collegiate-network.org. One feature, called the CN Syndicate, allows member papers to download articles from the web for printing in their own newspaper. The articles featured on the syndicate transcend their own local surroundings and often highlight instances of egregious political correctness.

In addition to the website, the CN also provides an internet discussion group. This forum provides editors from around the country with a quick and inexpensive way to obtain information, do research, share experiences, ask for advice, and discuss situations that arise on their campuses.

*Campus* magazine, a publication of the Intercollegiate Studies Institute written entirely by college students, was founded in 1990 to heighten public awareness of the problems that beset higher education. A national forum for CN writers, *Campus* offers the only national student voice opposing efforts to deny free-speech rights to those who do not follow the academic party line on curriculum reform, the politicization of the classroom, and declining educational standards. Each issue of *Campus* features a particular problem at America's colleges, such as campus crime, the curriculum crack-up, or the denial of due process in student tribunals. Each academic year, three issues, with a circulation of 125,000 copies each, are distributed on campuses nationwide. As an additional service, the Collegiate Network periodically sends articles, reports, studies, and federal documents to its members.

Collegiate Network student editors are talented, energetic, intelligent—they are the true leaders on America's campuses today. They have earned their stripes in the culture wars and have been granted CN membership. It's a mark of distinction.

## INVOLVING YOUR ALUMNI

Most of the initial funding for your publication will be generated through donations, so it is never too early to begin your outreach to that potentially huge source of financial and moral support: committed conservative alumni. The *Dartmouth Review,* with its 4,500 alumni paying $25 apiece for subscriptions, as well as numerous big donors, shows both ways of soliciting support. One method is to send a mailing to a list of alumni asking for a modest contribution in exchange for a subscription. A second way is to make personal contacts with alumni with the intent of receiving large contributions.

The problem with mail solicitation is that direct mailing generally does not produce good turnarounds. The professionals say that a 1-to-2-percent response to a mailing is typical.

Personal visits may be your more practical option, especially if your school is reluctant to divulge its mailing lists. The list you work with must be highly likely to produce good results. But if you can attract the interest of even one or two prominent wealthy and conservative alumni, you may be able to procure just such a list. Even then, however, the task ahead is formidable. Each personal visit takes time, and following up on that visit takes even more time.

In effect, personal solicitation is the pursuit of relationships with alumni. Relationships take time and cannot be neglected. Ideally, they will be preserved for many years after you have graduated. Successful relationship-building with alumni will consume large portions of your vacations and summers. It will also take time during the publishing year. But the successes of students like Peter Thiel, who raised $43,000 for the *Stanford Review* in this way, show that the effort is well worth making.

If you build relationships with a number of alumni donors, you may want to set up an alumni board for the publication. This not only formalizes your relationships; it makes their upkeep less problematic. By agreeing to serve on your alumni board, they expect you to call them on a regular basis.

You should not abuse the privilege, but an open line of communication with alumni can enable you to expand solicitations. For instance, a board member may agree to send a letter to other alumni who are likely to support the publication, on the member's letterhead, with his board title beneath his signature. Or the board may be able to intercede on your behalf with the administration to allow access to donor lists (even if only through the alumni magazine). The better your relations with connected alumni, the more connections you are likely to make.

One final caveat—your paper's name, your own name, and your intellectual property are all valuable commodities. Be aware of the protections that copyright law and intellectual property law afford you and your publication.

## PREPARING FOR YEAR TWO

Recruitment is key for the continued success of your publication. As you prepare for the new school year you should reread the section on recruitment. You need to recruit not only new staff, but new leaders. You will see the importance of the latter as the summer months approach, for summer is a time of great transitions. High school seniors emigrate to the nation's campuses, college graduates pass into the nation's workforce, and in the history of independent student publishing, summer has often been the time of failed transitions: of editors and publishers who graduated without grooming their successors, of computer gurus who quit the publication and took with them valuable technical skills, of ad salesmen who closed their portfolios for good instead of training others to pick up vital accounts. These are the sad stories of publications that did not go through that critical ritual of transition at the end of the school year, thus leaving the papers much poorer come autumn.

The time will soon come when you should think about passing *Start the Presses!* on to others—if not in your second year, then in your third or fourth. Pause during the first year of publication to remind yourself that this project you are working on is a vehicle for ideas. Your publication gives budding young conservative intellectuals and journalists a permanent home on your campus to develop their writing skills, an opportunity they would otherwise have been denied. That is a project worth sustaining.

Plan ahead, so someone else can succeed you at the paper, improve it, and gain more resources and knowledge than you had when the publication was still barely out of the womb. So that your successors can face bravely that second (or third or fourth) year in your publication's young life, you must prepare them for it. One cannot begin too early to identify and groom successors. If graduating seniors fill any leadership positions, they should scrutinize every new staff recruit for the possibility of assuming a post in the spring semester. Until the time of actual transition, those in leadership should work with their successors, teaching their skills and imparting acquired wisdom.

◆ One extremely useful tool to be used during this ritual of transition is a set of *written guidelines* regarding the day-to-day operations of the enterprise. Late in the first year of publication, each member of the leadership team should write a section for an in-house handbook that includes a brief job description of each leadership position, important details to be retained (technical specifications, vendors and order numbers frequently used, etc.), and lessons learned from experience. The editor in chief, for instance, would want to commit the production schedule to writing and explain each of his editors' roles in putting out a typical issue. The publisher would want to list all major alumni contributors, give advice on relations with each, and similarly explain how to deal with the printer, the post office, and so on. Each member of the new leadership team should get a copy of this handbook.

◆ Another invaluable written resource is the publication's archives. You should put a copy of each issue in a binder and at the end of the year permanently bind the issues into a reference volume. Future writers and editors will refer to these pages again and again for story ideas, design tips, and factual verification.

◆ If a number of the paper's alumni will continue to live in the vicinity of campus after they graduate, they might want to consider forming an alumni board of trustees for the publication. While it need not have any formal powers, such a board would be yet another resource for future editors. The advisory role of the founders and subsequent alumni of the alternative publication is unique not only in the field of journalism but, outside of the fraternity system, has no parallel anywhere on campus. Several CN publications have utilized a board of alumni. Their presence will remind their successors of the commitment to the independent views that got the publication started in the first place.

## HANDLING CONTROVERSY

Sit-ins for "social justice." Marches to "take back the night." Hunger strikes for "peace" in some Third World country you've never heard of. Vigils for "animal rights." Protests against "globalization."

Ho-hum stuff on today's college campus. Sure, the editors at your campus daily are fascinated with these events the campus Left sponsors *ad nauseam*. Five shaggy students chant about the cause *du jour*, show up at a "demonstration" with scribbled slogans on $1.99 poster board, and your campus daily has reporters on the scene recording anguished quotes for a contrived story the next day. This is called street theater. It is not news.

You and most other students at your university have tired of such antics. You even work on a campus newspaper that combats these radicals and their dangerous ideas. Yet, in their fevered activity lurks the gem of an idea, and the staff of your newspaper can learn something from the protesters. Though their ideas are anathema, their tactics in attracting media attention have been wonderfully successful.

If you generate public controversy, you, too, can expect media attention. If people see that you and your staff are doing much more than writing high-minded treatises on the latest international crisis and are actually causing a stir, your paper could attract more donations, staff, and subscriptions. You might even become a local celebrity.

There are two kinds of controversies that Collegiate Network newspapers experience. The first is the controversy that you planned, that you generated, that you expected. The second is the controversy that catches you offguard. Typically, this latter happens when you write something in your newspaper that you assume is harmless but that offends the sensibilities of self-anointed campus leaders. For instance, the *California Review* at the University of California at San Diego found itself in a controversy when the members of the student senate objected to a graphic in an issue of the *Review* that depicted a scene from the Spanish Inquisition. These senators said it resembled slavery and was therefore "offensive."

Whatever the controversy, the most important thing to do is to go to the media with your side of the story. Write a press release—no more than one page—and fax it to your daily newspapers, to your local newspaper, to the Collegiate Network, to the *Chronicle of Higher Education*, to syndicated columnists. *Get your story out.* Don't think that because it's a local issue national media won't care; maybe what's going on is part of a national pattern.

Let's take an example. Say you're a student at the University of Honolulu and the student congress has just voted that, in order to atone for America's use of atomic weapons in World War II, Japanese students at the university will receive first pick of on-campus housing. The prevailing wisdom—which the university's administration, faculty, and student journalists accept—is that only such a move can help to heal the fifty-year-old wounds that have been festering since America unjustly and illegally dropped the atomic bomb.

What do you, the editor of the *Honolulu Spectator*, do?

The wrong answer is to write letters to the director of university housing and respectfully request that the student congress's vote be ignored. A similar wrong answer is to wait three weeks until your next issue comes out to write a philosophical argument against preferential racial treatment in university housing.

You should act now. Here are several possibilities:

◆ Hold a "Rally Against Racism" outside student government offices. Call the proposed housing policy what it is: a racist segregation of students. Do not argue the merits of dropping atomic weapons. That is irrelevant to the debate. It happened fifty years ago. If you argue that issue, you are allowing your opponents to frame the debate, and you will lose. The question is, Should the university divide students by race? Why should students who have not been victims of atomic attack receive benefits at the expense of students who have not attacked anyone with atomic weapons?

At the rally, march and chant with picket signs. Be creative, and don't feel stupid or that what you're doing is ridiculous. Sure, the activities might feel childish, but college students have been doing this for decades. Take a Mercedes hood ornament, draw a vertical line through it, and you have the conscience of a generation forever captured on T-shirts and bumper stickers. Think of your paper as generating visually stunning images for the evening news.

A couple of suggestions: a "Down With Student Internment!!" picket sign, perhaps with a drawing of a student behind bars. Another sign that says: "The Real Bomb: Student Government's Racist Housing Plot!!!" Exclamation points show anger and excitement (in signs only). Use lots of them. If your signs are inflammatory enough, left-wing activists will argue with you and denounce you in the press. This is good, as you have distracted them from their mission of obtaining preferential housing.

◆ Send press releases to news organizations. Fax them, preferably in the morning when reporters are scrounging for news. The daily hunt for news is dreary, and if you can craft a press release that promises excitement, reporters are more likely to cover your event.

If you hold a rally, hype it in the press release. The press release should succinctly discuss the issue and highlight conflict. Reporters love conflict. The more of it, the better. The press release should be no longer than one page. Remember that the purpose of a press release, like a Pavlovian bell, is to get the subject interested in what you're doing. Few reporters actually quote from press releases.

To aid reporters, include contact names and phone numbers of people they can call to get the story. Include yourselves, of course, but also include your opponents: the leftist activists leading the charge, the student government officers, and university officials. The reporter will contact these people anyway, but you have made his task easier by saving him a trip to the phone book. You also increase the chances of your opponents getting unexpected calls from reporters. This creates a panicked sense among your opponents that things are spinning out of their control.

In talking to the press, know what you're going to say beforehand. Speak slowly, as most reporters struggle to jot down everything you say. Prepare a few sound bites, and say these first. In response to a reporter's question about why you are opposed to the policy, you might say, "Jim, in the interests of racial justice, it is important that we be open-minded and not allow ourselves to return to the ugly past of segregation and racial conflict." Note the use of traditionally left-wing terms such as "racial justice" and "open-minded" in new contexts. When possible, use these kinds of terms ("dialogue," "bridge-building," "awareness"). Who can object to dialogue or justice?

♦ Contact alumni and state legislators. If you know any prominent alumni, let them know what is happening on campus. Ask them to write letters to the administration expressing their concern over the proposed policy. Most administrators are not knee-jerk liberals. They simply take the path of least resistance, and usually they do not find resistance along liberal paths. But if you can enlist alumni in your effort—either a significant number of alumni or a few alums who donate big money to the university—administrators will take notice. The last thing the university wants is for its funding sources to dry up because of a stupid debate over housing policy.

If you attend a public university, state legislators can help. Like alumni, state legislators provide funding to the university. And it's not their money: it's the taxpayers' money. Why should taxpayer money be used to enforce segregation in campus housing? Pitch it like that to friendly legislators. They might find a campaign issue, and you might find some help and an ongoing contact in state government.

Once you have deployed these tactics, continue them until the issue is resolved. Keep talking to the press and ensure that your point of view gets in the papers. The coverage of you and your efforts might not always be flattering, but remember that at least your viewpoint is in the paper. Without you, it wouldn't be.

Also, you will probably be targeted for personal attacks. People will question your motives, call you a racist and other unsettling names. Don't worry about it. Most people recognize personal attacks for what they really are: cheap, inflammatory rhetoric from someone who can't argue substance. The first time you are slandered publicly as "racist" or "homophobic" or whatever, it may be pretty heavy. By sophomore year, you'll laugh it off as the routine cynical ploy it is. And you have the ultimate campus weapon with which to fight back—your own newspaper.

The real dividends for the *Honolulu Spectator* come after some of the dust has settled on the controversy. By now, you've probably written about the housing issue in your paper, and you've probably been quoted in the local media. Take those clippings and mail them to donors and potential donors. They will be pleased that you are doing more than writing hurried essays late at night in a cramped dorm room for a paper thousands of issues smaller than the campus daily. If you send press clips to them, it shows that you are having an impact. It shows that you are, to borrow another liberal phrase, working for change on campus.

Remember that you speak for most of the students at the University of Honolulu. They are simply afraid to voice their real thoughts for fear of offending the cabal of students, faculty, and administrators who run the place. You aren't afraid, and your actions prove it.

Along with the press clips, send a letter recounting what you've done and ask for money so that the *Honolulu Spectator* can continue its efforts to reform the university. With more money, you can publish more pages or publish more frequently to get your message out.

The controversy might also have attracted new staff members to your publication. When the campus powers-that-be tried to smear the *Carolina Review* at the University of North Carolina with bogus charges of anti-Semitism, numerous students saw the scam for what it was and joined the *Review* staff. They were unfamiliar with the *Review* previously, but the controversy—

along with the *Review's* in-your-face response—put the paper on the front page of the campus daily for several consecutive days. You can't buy that kind of publicity.

Don't run from controversy. Don't cower and hope it goes away. Respond to it on *your* terms, and take your case to the public through the local media, alumni, and others who can help you.

As the editor of an alternative campus paper, you might often think that yours is the minority view. But you'll find that more people agree with you than you think.

# MANIPULATING CONTROVERSY TO YOUR ADVANTAGE

**By Marc Levin**
Editor Emeritus, *Austin Review*

Controversy is a perennial staple of journalism, and it is arguably even more vital to an alternative conservative campus publication. While students may reflexively pick up the official school paper to get the latest sports scores and entertainment listings, they often need an extra incentive to pick up a more infrequently published conservative newspaper or magazine. A touch of controversy can provide that extra incentive.

The kinds of subjects and issues that are likely to be controversial on campus can vary over time. One rule is that local stories will stimulate more controversy than national ones. For example, an article exposing improprieties on the part of the university president will generate more reaction than a similar article dealing with the president of the United States. Also, issues like affirmative action, multiculturalism, gay rights, animal rights, abortion, and student fees will be more controversial on campus than agricultural policy and electricity deregulation. While it can be argued that the latter two issues also affect students, the former issues tend to elicit a visceral reaction from people while the latter ones, even if important, do not.

If you have difficulty coming up with controversial story ideas for your publication, you might consider an evergreen approach. For example, a list of the best and worst professors and classes is always a winner, and you can run it anytime.

Once you have controversial stories in the hopper, you want to squeeze the most from them. Several strategies can help to maximize the controversial punch your paper delivers. First, images add color to controversy. For example, a picture of chanting campus leftists, accompanied by an article debunking their claims, can be highly effective. For some articles, such as a story exposing a display of sexually explicit artwork on campus, pictures are indispensable. A clear picture of the artwork accomplishes more than a lengthy description. Second, the impact of controversial stories is maximized by placing them on the front page. Don't run a book review or another ponderous piece on the front page when you have a story on the inside that exposes a campus scandal.

Finally, good headlines are critical to exploiting controversial stories. While headlines should not mislead, they should do everything possible to draw the reader to the story. For instance, the *Austin Review* ran the headline "A Brief History of Light Rail in Austin." While that title is accurate, it is more appropriate for a historical journal than a newspaper. Headlines should include strong action verbs and subjects such as the president of the university, the student government, etc., that students are familiar with and care about.

In your efforts to generate controversial stories, avoid pitfalls. First, don't simply repeat or repackage reporting done in the official school paper. Unless the students at the official campus paper have their heads in the sand, they will report on most campus controversies. This still leaves you with two avenues for weighing in on these controversies to stimulate interest in your conservative publication. Ideally, through investigative reporting, you can uncover some new information that the official school paper missed, or you can reveal some new angle on the story. If this is not possible, you can write an editorial. For example, if there are protests on campus against sweatshops, your editorial might shed new light on the subject by applying the free market economic perspective, which likely was absent in the official student paper's coverage.

Another pitfall can arise if your publication itself becomes the source of controversy. While this is always uncomfortable, it can be either good or bad depending on how you handle it. Suppose that your publication exposes how certain professors of questionable competence were hired because of a racial quota, and these professors then launch a public attack on your paper, threatening to sue. As long as your facts are accurate, you have nothing to fear. Remember to stay away from personal attacks or "revelations" about your opponents except as they relate to public performance. This is a distinction between a "public" and "private" person, which is central to the application of libel law.

If it is available, taking a course in media law and ethics will enable you to make better informed decisions regarding the publication of controversial material. Short of taking a course, consider checking out a book on this subject from the library. The *Associated Press Stylebook and Libel Manual* is an excellent resource. You will learn valuable tips about the basics of libel law, respect for intellectual property, and the responsibilities that journalists have to the truth.

If you do commit a snafu, such as wrongly accusing someone of something, it is best to quickly admit your mistake, issue an apology, and run a prominent correction. This helps rehabilitate the credibility of your paper and reduces your chance of being held legally liable. In some states, the law even allows media outlets to escape liability by issuing an apology and a correction. On the other hand, if you have the facts right and the issue is more ideological than personal, don't commit the error of apologizing or backing down simply because campus leftists are furious with your paper and threatening a lawsuit. Instead, as long as you have not committed libel, the fact that campus leftists are angry with your paper should be viewed as a badge of honor and a sign that you are doing your job. After all, this is far better than your paper's dwelling in obscurity because it is not controversial.

While publishing controversial stories can make you unpopular within some quarters on campus and lead to threats of a lawsuit, such stories are crucial if your goal is to make a significant impact. Although thoughtful expositions on conservative philosophy and reviews of the latest books and public policy studies are not without merit, these stories will not yield the front page headlines that cut through the campus clutter and lead a student to pick up your paper. While stories that are heavier on philosophy than controversy can be accommodated on the inside pages of your publication, these pieces will not accomplish anything if people do not pick up your publication in the first place. Viewed in this way, controversy is a tool for encouraging students to learn about conservative ideas. Since this is your ultimate goal, it becomes clear why controversy must become grist for your paper's mill.

## How to Hold a Successful Event

**By Morgan N. Knull**
Founder, *Wabash Commentary*

During my four years in college, every leftist sideshow working the university circuit seemed to pull into campus. There was the Mexican-American "performance artist" who, wearing only underwear and boots, squashed chicken carcasses on stage while shouting Spanish obscenities at the audience. The colorful parade of charlatans included one speaker who declared that Martin Luther King "was assassinated by forces deep from within the Pentagon." Unchallenged by an audience that included the dean of students and the college president, he chanted, "The Holocaust is coming!"

Yet most conservatives today realize that if any campus inferno is raging, it involves the "deconstruction" of our culture and history. While leftists prattle about "diversity," rarely do they invite speakers who dissent from their own party line.

The dilemma for independent papers is not whether more conservative speakers are needed or might find an audience on campus. You know they would. The question is how to sponsor a speaking event without breaking your group's budget and your own back.

Begin by compiling a little empirical evidence of bias in existing institutional lecture programs. Most schools sponsor a visiting lecture series, and many also have faculty committees or departments that organize events. Student government may have its own program and use mandatory student fees to fund it.

It takes only a few hours to produce a list of speakers who have been invited in recent years by these groups to lecture. Back issues of the campus newspaper usually are available in the library or online and can be a good source of information. Schools publish lecture calendars. If your paper is well established, look through its coverage of past speakers.

Once the list is compiled, analyze the speakers and lecture topics. Does any pattern emerge? What is the ratio of liberal to conservative lectures in a given period of time? How much money was spent and what was its source?

A less extensive sampling consists of examining past commencement speakers and honorary degree recipients. Have fading liberal celebrities and socialist political activists dominated?

Use this information to justify the need to solicit and spend money to sponsor a lecture. Your paper already brings alternative ideas to campus. Rhetorically frame the lecture not as a righteous crusade to proclaim truth (though it probably is) but as a simple desire to spark campus debate and restore balance. Talk about the need for "a marketplace of ideas."

Next, identify several liberal lectures that featured particularly egregious quotes or details. A speaker's claim that the CIA is assassinating key American politicians, for instance, will help persuade many alumni and supporters that balance must be restored. Several horrifying anecdotes should complement the empirical data you collect.

When you have built a convincing case that institutional offerings do not provide for a balance of viewpoints, identify the issues pertinent to your campus. Is a particular subject being hotly debated? Has a recent controversial speaker or action ignited the campus? Issues such as affirmative action, feminism, and censorship typically inspire interest and strong emotions.

Selecting a subject requires savvy and familiarity with the campus pulse. Illegal immigration is unlikely to be a hot topic in Iowa, but it is in California. If your campus is debating a speech code or multiculturalist proposal, a lecture on the subject is timely. Political issues find the largest audience when talks coincide with upcoming ballot initiatives or elections.

Establish a list of several possible speakers and contact them. Will they speak on the desired topic? What are the available dates? How much are their honoraria and travel expenses?

The basic rule: the better known a speaker is, the more he charges and the larger the audience he will attract. If he has ties to your school or a passion for the subject, he may reduce or waive his expenses. In election years, candidates from your district and state should readily accept invitations, especially if you live in a competitive presidential primary state.

Before formalizing an event, consider how much name recognition a speaker has, what subject he will speak on, how much he will cost, and the size of the audience you seek. Will the result justify the effort? What is the fundraising potential?

Several conservative foundations, including the Intercollegiate Studies Institute, run speakers bureaus. In some cases, they provide partial financial support. Explore the possibilities.

Once you are ready to proceed, fully integrate the event into your paper's coverage and activities. Send a fundraising appeal to subscribers and explain the bias in official campus lectures using facts to illustrate the need for balance. Invite them to attend and ask for their financial support.

Approach the student government and insist that it practice fairness by contributing toward the lecture. If you know of sympathetic trustees, alumni, or community members, contact them for assistance. A private dinner or reception should be organized for prominent speakers, and you can sell tickets or use it as a perquisite for big donors.

In large towns, assemble a lecture program and solicit advertising from businesses and local politicians. On some campuses, individual departments or other student groups will cosponsor lectures. The goal is not only to meet your budget but to increase attendance by involving more people.

Promote the lecture in your paper. Run an advance interview or publish a profile on the speaker. Monitor campus reaction; attempts to obstruct the lecture should be publicized because these will generate support and boost attendance. After the speech, run excerpts or a follow-up story on the evening.

While seeking to restore balance to campus debate, do not forget to balance your own speaking program. At Wabash College, our magazine hosted lectures on a variety of topics ranging from welfare reform to multiculturalism to talk radio. In one year, we sponsored separate events featuring a conservative alumnus, a candidate for statewide office, a nun who ran a homeless shelter, the executive director of the state ACLU, and economist and columnist Thomas Sowell.

Sponsoring lectures will enhance your paper's credibility, expand the readership and base of supporters, and create a buzz around campus. They are a positive and needed contribution that provides the marketplace of ideas most schools promise but fail to deliver.

# GOING DIGITAL: BUILDING A WEBSITE FOR YOUR PUBLICATION

By Wesley Wynne
Founder, *Contumacy*

## THE VALUE OF GOING ONLINE

With a website, the potential audience for your publication becomes literally worldwide. Unlike print copies, online editions can't be stolen by politically correct vandals or confiscated by irate college administrators. Other advantages abound. The costs of web publishing are low. Basic web skills are not difficult to learn, and a website can serve in a terrific supplementary role to your print edition.

## HOW TO DO IT

Decide early whether you want your site to be hosted on your school's web server, or on a third party's. Most universities now allow student organizations to have web space free of charge. But with this gift comes control. Political entanglements that could lead to censorship of your paper could also lead to censorship of your website. The alternative of getting an account through an outside internet service provider or web hosting service may be preferable and could cost as little as $20 per month. Another advantage to going off-campus with your web service is having your own internet address. An internet address is simple to register and inexpensive (under $100 for two years). It is also much more elegant and desirable:
*www.contumacy.com* is easier to remember and advertise than *www.utexas.edu/students/orgs/contumacy.html*.

You need two basic skill sets to construct and maintain a good site: design savvy and computer know-how. Chances are, if you are good at print design, you'll be good at web design; and most papers already have a print designer who can guide website layout. If you need design ideas, review the websites of other student publications. The Collegiate Network provides a list of its members' websites at www.collegiate-network.org. Begin there.

After you determine basic site layout, the rest of the design work can consist of routine updating. For that, and for the rest of the computer maintenance, you need someone with technical skills. This includes knowledge of basic HTML or mastery of web editing applications such as Microsoft's FrontPage or Macromedia's Dreamweaver. It also includes a working knowledge of Adobe Photoshop or other image editing programs, the ability to upload new content, and the capacity to troubleshoot various computer problems. It isn't rocket science, but it takes patience and effort to master these skills. Finding someone who already has experience might be easier that having a current staff member start from scratch. Over the past few years, however, software developers have taken much of the wizardry out of web publishing by producing tools that do some of the magic for you.

## Maintaining and Expanding Your Site

Once your site is up, what should you do with it? Three words: keep it current.

To get the maximum benefit from the web, you must update your site regularly with new content. One popular way to do this is to have a parallel web edition for each print edition you publish. Set deadlines for updating the content of your web edition.

In addition to the editorial content, your site should contain information on subscriptions and recruiting, a staff list, and information on how to advertise with your publication. You may want to include an archive of back issues. Keeping in mind that the web is interactive, place the e-mail addresses of your authors alongside their bylines. Consider adding other features eventually, such as search engines, a discussion forum, chat rooms, etc.

For maximum impact, advertise your web address both on the cover of and inside your print edition. If you post fliers around campus for your paper (a good idea), be sure to include your web address there, too. You might also want to offer supplemental information exclusively online. For example, you can make complete interview transcripts available, publish pertinent legal documents in their entirety, and add full-color images to accompany your text. Your audience will grow once the visitors to your site discover that you offer additional content online.

Websites are already regarded as essential by many publications and will become even more so in the future. For papers keeping up with the times, a web presence is now almost a given. Fortunately, the tools and effort needed to establish a good site are no longer the province of the expert.

# The CN's Impact

**By Jeffrey R. Giesea**
Former Editor, *Stanford Review*

Consider the evidence: Matthew Rees fights at the vanguard of the conservative movement as an editorial staff member of the *Weekly Standard*. He previously wrote for the *Wall Street Journal* in Europe. After stints at the *New Republic* and the *New York Post*, Jonathan Karl transferred to CNN, where he serves as news correspondent extraordinaire. Wendy Shalit, a 1998 Williams College graduate, has already published articles in national publications, served as contributing editor of the Manhattan Institute's *City Journal,* and published a successful book, *A Return to Modesty*. David Mastio keeps the "Motor City" thinking right at the *Detroit News*, Washington Bureau. And Matthew Robinson ensures that education issues get adequate coverage in *Investor's Business Daily*, where he is a reporter.

These young, rising stars in the national media share a common bond. All are alumni of the Collegiate Network. Their successes confirm that CN graduates are an emerging force in the media.

Mr. Karl, Mr. Rees, Ms. Shalit, Mr. Mastio and Mr. Robinson are just a few of the professional journalists and authors the CN has spawned. Many others picked up valuable skills and insight through experience with CN publications—Rhodes, Marshall, and Fulbright scholars; prominent lawyers, doctors, and investment bankers; and rising politicians, policymakers, and professors. Then there are the innumerable readers of CN publications who saw the principles of a free society convincingly applied to campus issues and now apply the same issue to all political matters.

The CN vastly aided my work as editor of the *Stanford Review*. The active internet discussion group gave me easily accessed eyes and ears on every campus with a CN publication. For example, when a reporter was trying to examine race-based financial aid policies at other schools, I e-mailed the editors' list, asking about their schools' financial aid policies regarding race; not long after, I received a flood of responses that proved invaluable to the reporter writing the article.

At the CN editors training conference I attended, the speakers shared useful and motivational advice, and the crowd of like-minded editors, each advancing the cause of liberty under hostile conditions, provided moral strength for our sometimes lonely battle. Additionally, I developed fresh ideas for articles, headlines, and layout designs from the other CN papers mailed to me.

I also benefited from other CN offerings, aside from those that foster communication among publications. For one thing, without the CN's assistance, I never could have helped fund and organize an on-campus affirmative action debate between Jesse Jackson and Dinesh D'Souza several weeks before the vote on the California Civil Rights Amendment. Nor would I have received effective recruitment tips from an experienced CN advisor, or learned about internship opportunities. Indeed, without the CN, my editorship would have been much more difficult and less fulfilling. I know most other CN participants feel the same way, especially those who owe the continued existence of their publications to the CN.

With all the support the CN provides, the success of its member publications is not surprising. The pages of CN publications have consistently chronicled the increase of politicized classes and departments, the questionable uses of mandatory student fees, the chilling effect of speech codes and campus hypersensitivity, and the countless other problematic characteristics of today's college campuses. The findings have trickled out to alumni, the national media, and the general public. The outcome: CN participants are shaping the terms of debate surrounding higher education.

CN publications are impacting the state of higher education. Despite these successes, much work remains; colleges and universities continue to decline under politically correct agendas.

Imagine a day when a CN publication sheds light on every college campus in this country.

# 6. TROUBLE SITUATIONS

AFTER A PUBLICATION cranks out several issues and settles into the routine of its first year of operation, new challenges will crop up, and with them a whole new set of questions. Some may concern situations that threaten to shipwreck your new paper. Others are related to the often painful, always rewarding process of growing as a visible force on campus. The following situations highlight general types of difficulties encountered by alternative publications on campuses, as you will see from the answers given.

## RIGHT-WING CONSPIRACIES

*A reporter for the campus daily wants to write a feature on us. As we were setting up an interview time on the phone, he asks us if we were being supported by any conservative foundations. I don't know this person, but I get the feeling he's not going to be friendly toward us. What should I tell him in the interview?*

*The president of the student government association has just called a de-recognition hearing for our publication. He accuses us of fronting for the national Republican Party, which would be a violation of the rule that says an official student group can't engage in political advocacy. How should we defend ourselves?*

The tax law that forbids political advocacy is both very specific and very open to interpretation. The specific prohibitions are mostly against lobbying practices. But lobbying is not "educational activity," which is allowed by the law. The latter category is where your publication resides in its entirety—in theory. The vagueness arises because the law doesn't specifically detail all activity that is "lobbying." Thus the battle is to demonstrate that everything you do is educational, not political.

The best defense is to snuff out the conspiracy theory at both ends. First, point to your editorial content. Note that all of it (or most of it) is locally written, by registered students, not by party hacks on a national payroll. If people start to question the CN's involvement, simply pull out recent issues of other publications in the Network that differ most widely from yours. Anybody who looks at the *Dartmouth Review,* the *Princeton Tory,* the *Virginia Advocate*, and the *Harvard Salient* would realize that the notion of these publications serving as mouthpieces for a single political interest is ridiculous.

Second, note the diversity of your funding. CN grants probably account for half of your annual income. About half will be from donors and advertising. Student government reps and reporters would like nothing better than for you to provide a list of every merchant who has advertised with you and the total amount paid by each, followed by the names and contributions of each alumnus, and finally the CN grant amount. Do not do this. It's no one's business but yours.

Remember the importance of having some variety in your editorial and news formats, including nonpolitical campus features. This has the double effect of attracting more readers and helping to dispel the conspiracy theories.

## SCHOOL VS. STUDENTS

*We have a well-known radical professor on our campus and would like to do a story critical of him. Unfortunately, some of our staff must take a required course with him this year, and they are urging us to avoid attacks. He has already been attacking us and has given a hard time to our staff. They are afraid he will flunk them outright. Should we go ahead anyway?*

*The alumni office just called to inform me they were not amused by our recent fundraising efforts to alumni (we don't know how they found out about it). They want to know where we got our list of names and everyone that we've contacted. But I compiled those names from lists not published by the university and through my alumni contacts. What can they do to me?*

The first rule in dealing with anyone at your school who is not just passing through en route to graduation is tread carefully but boldly. Faculty, administrators, and school bureaucrats all have the power to make life miserable for your publication. Some of them will not choose this route either because they don't care or because they believe they will outlast you anyway. Still others, however, may really try to run you out of town. Yet to do that they would need support from their less interested colleagues. Thus your strategy is to keep potentially explosive situations from developing or, if they are inevitable, to ensure that the fireworks go off in their backyard, not yours.

This means you treat professors, all professors, with professional respect. There are published guidelines for dealing with faculty, and you ought to be familiar with your school's regulations. This includes rules on auditing a course (you may not be able to just "sit in" on a session or two), tape recording, and complaint procedures. In addition, schools are increasingly developing "sensitivity guidelines," which are much vaguer but are intended to shield professors entirely from criticism (although such guidelines are usually advanced with the argument that they are meant to shield students). You may not like these codes, but you must know them and creatively find a way around them.

Here is where a *faculty advisor* can be your best friend in times of trouble. Most alternative publications find a tenured professor who is friendly toward the publication and willing to serve as advisor. Your faculty advisor should receive a standing invitation to all leadership meetings and staff socials. He can give you new insight into a controversy, including the backgrounds of those people involved and the way the judicial processes work at your school. He can also tell you when a story you are considering running hits below the belt or makes too-sweeping charges against the faculty.

Finally, remember that the best cure is prevention. Cultivate informal ties with faculty and administrators; if you need friends-in-high-places, you can turn to them. And above all, never forget the double standard. Stories that do not hold to the moral high ground at all times on sensitive issues are stories that invite retaliation. Good stories won't necessarily prevent such attacks, but they will greatly diminish your enemies' ammunition supply.

## Students vs. Students

*Well, it happened. Sometime during the morning that we distributed our last issue, the stacks began vanishing around campus. We found a few of them in nearby waste cans. Most of them are simply gone. We will write a letter to the dean of students, and get a sympathetic senator to suggest disciplinary regulations at the next student government meeting, but we're not holding our breath that either of these actions will do much, especially since we don't have any witnesses. So now what?*

*We are starting an alternative monthly magazine at a small college. The community here is very tightly knit and politically conscious, but not in a way that favors us. We think that if we try even to suggest a different perspective on some controversial issues, we'll be shut down immediately, and by public acclamation to boot. How do we minimize the emotional reaction without sacrificing our principles?*

Situations like these remind you just how lonely a venture political journalism can be at some schools. If you have the tenacity to survive on your campus, however, you need not fear isolation, as long as you responsibly go it alone.

Every publication, when it is starting up, should take seriously the idea that it is an open forum for a variety of conservative and other opinions. As Ronald Reagan once said during the 1980 primaries, when the sound at his podium was turned off, "Hey, I paid for this microphone!" Likewise, as long as you pay the bills, you control who gets to express their views on your pages. Even if you decide to print an "opposing views" column, the point is, it is *your* column. You can decide to leave it alone or to pair it with a counterpoint column. It is your microphone. By inviting a few different voices to speak into it, you can attract a wider audience and, more importantly, allow the enemy to vent his spleen on *your* turf instead of his. But it remains *your* choice.

Another way to dispel reaction before it can gather steam is to welcome criticism of articles already published. Your letters-to-the-editor policy should be very generous: try to print as many letters as you can and do not edit the text unless the letter greatly exceeds the guideline, which is usually 300 words.

Hand-in-hand with welcoming criticism is admitting when you are wrong. Professional papers do it every day. You may wish to run something a little larger and less insulting-looking than the corrections space that papers usually bury on page 2.

The instance of vandalism should reinforce something noted above in the second point, namely that a good knowledge of the rules at your school is essential. You shouldn't distribute where distribution is expressly forbidden, unless you are willing to conduct surveillance, because that will weaken your case when you complain about stolen papers. Even if you can guard your issues, you can't do much about an administrator who issues a new edict to stop you. A better route is to know the rules and, where potential difficulties exist, try to get around them.

When vandalism occurs, use all channels of complaint—even if they appear futile—and above all, raise a stink about it on the front page of your next issue. Prepare a press release, and fax it to local and national media contacts. Include names and contact phone numbers. Make this a news story; this will encourage you to start your own investigation and to get information about the incident on the record. If your next issue won't come out for a while, complain about the vandalism in a letter to the editor of the establishment paper. As long as you keep it a live issue, either you will help discourage further thefts or, if thefts continue, your stories will generate support for your publication.

## Trouble at the Top

*Our editor in chief just quit. He had been doing too much for the publication as it was; he had a hard time delegating duties. Now we've sold a bunch of advertising for an issue that's supposed to come out in two weeks. Also, he owned the computer we used all the time, and did all the desktop publishing. He insisted on doing everything on the computer and didn't teach us anything. Do we cancel the issue?*

Again, think prevention. We have already discussed transition, but it bears repeating: A publication that is not ready to pass its operations to a new leadership by the end of its first year is no more ready to handle the sudden departure of anyone in its current leadership. To avoid either unfortunate outcome means spreading leadership around to develop new leaders. One idea that has worked for many publications was mentioned in "Second Steps": having a board of directors that meets occasionally with the current editors to discuss problems and instill in them the institutional memory of the publication. In the event of an editor's unexpected resignation, the knowledge of past editors could make all the difference in continuing a publication.

A related hazard is a clique mentality at the top: symptoms include editors who won't share knowledge about their jobs with noneditors, who do not follow up on every potential recruit that contacts them, or who generally give the impression of a too-closely-knit fraternity.

If a breakdown in the leadership makes publishing the next issue on time impossible, decide on a make-up date (make it sooner rather than later), get to your advertisers quickly, explain the situation, and see if they will accept the new date. Be responsible businessmen, treat your advertisers with all the courtesy due your embarrassment, and you might even win new respect from them.

## Trouble with Staff

*We've recruited a few staff who are not conservative. The founding editors, who are graduating, are concerned about appointing students who are not conservative to positions of leadership. These students have worked hard for the publication, but are not committed to conservative principles. Should they be turned away?*

While there is certainly a diversity of opinion among conservatives on various issues, your paper must stand firm for a core set of values or beliefs. This is where the mission statement can help. When recruiting, you should ask potential staffers whether they feel comfortable with the positions that the paper takes. If not, then perhaps they should write for the official school paper.

There are positions on the paper—advertising and distribution—that do not require one to be conservative. However, one should be careful about bringing such people aboard, as their motive could be sabotage of your operation. If a student is politically apathetic and wants to make a few extra dollars selling advertisements, then you may want to bring him aboard the staff.

One should be careful though when filling positions of leadership. Your paper is not in the business of being "diverse." While your publication is concerned with the truth, it is also concerned with propounding a particular worldview and set of ideas that most Americans find salutary. Beware of the student who wants to turn your paper into a "forum for the exchange of ideas." That's the university's job—your job is to provide the ideas.

## A Question of Expertise

*In three weeks, the faculty committee holds a vote on whether to replace the existing core curriculum with a new one that is more "diversified"—i.e., Third World. The whole process seems very secretive, although we did obtain a list of the proposed courses and assigned readings. We want to expose this sham, but none of us are experts on higher education. How can we say as much without getting in over our heads?*

Reporters are constantly called upon to report on matters they initially know little about. Those who do a good job accumulate an impressive pile of research and organize it in time to meet their deadlines. They write transparently, using direct quotes and paraphrases, letting the interpretations of others, rather than their own, shape the story. In other words, it's not so important to have expertise. You must, however, have the skill of reading and distilling the experts.

You can start developing this skill now in three ways. The first is to cultivate contacts. Your friends on the faculty can offer background and direct you to primary sources of information when a story arises in their field. ISI's Collegiate Network is a good friend to have, too; most likely the story you are investigating has already appeared elsewhere and the CN knows about it, or knows of other schools where the alternative publication, or a renowned professor, could supply expertise.

Second, learn to write using the voices of others. The cultural diversity issue is a good one to cut your teeth on because of the abundance of excellent fresh material available on the subject. Get some background on the subject from recently published books and articles. Call the CN; we may even know of a source that's specific to your school's situation. Next, identify a professor of English or literature who will give you a "local angle." Then draw on your own experience. It is possible for you to state your opinions on the curriculum debate because, like most issues on your campus, it involves you. Not arguing over your head means more than just saying everyone should read the ancient Greeks. Cite authors whose works you have read and explain why you found reading them to be an invaluable experience. It may not be expertise of the first order, but it can personalize and lend weight to your story.

Third, treat big stories appropriately: write follow-up stories, invite criticism, and admit it if you've made a big goof in your argumentation. The voices of the experts do not speak unanimously, and sometimes it takes more than one treatment to report a big issue in all its depth and complexity. When the reader can understand the controversy in all its dimensions, your point of view comes across emphatically.

## Sensitive Issues and Boycotts

*The local chapter of the statewide gay task force got wind of an article on homosexuals in our last issue. We thought it was a good piece, strongly worded, and responsible. Now the gays are planning to publicize a boycott of all our advertisers. They plan to picket storefronts and demand that the merchants sign their petition. Are we in trouble or what?*

Boycotts are the sometimes unavoidable reactions to stories you publish on sensitive issues on your campus, such as homosexuality, racial issues, or feminism. Where they are in fact unavoidable, you can survive with your finances intact. But first, a word about ensuring that any boycott leveled against your publication is only the "unavoidable" type.

Sensitive issues require particular agility with the facts. The threat of an organized reaction to articles you might run on sensitive issues shouldn't scare you away from writing them, but should help ensure that these stories are scrupulously reported and argued.

First, the facts should be the heart of the publication and the argument peripheral, not the other way around. A writer who simply spins off his reflections on an article he just read in the daily about a gay students' rally is not putting the facts first.

Second, in gathering information for your stories, be sure to get the other side of the story. This means going to the sources and understanding their rationale well enough that you can give their side as well as they could. For instance, if you are scrutinizing the black student organization, you should get an interview with one or several of those involved in it, including at least one of its leaders. You may find that covering sensitive issues as *news* stories rather than as opinion pieces will allow you to better present the argument you are opposing. This, of course, will make the presentation more complex, and your argument will appear perhaps subtler and less strident.

Third, and above all, remember to attack the argument, not the person stating it. This is especially difficult to do if you are writing on issues of personal lifestyle, but it is a valuable skill to learn if you wish to be more persuasive than the emotional opposition.

Here again the importance of opening your forum to criticism can't be overstated. When you run a story on a sensitive issue, brace yourself for hate mail and then print all of it. A point-counterpoint running in the same issue could also defuse tensions.

Sometimes, however, you will be unable to find writers for both sides, and while waiting to publish the letters reacting to your story, a boycott—an unavoidable one—is organized against your advertisers. *Act quickly.* Get to every media outlet you can with your story. An editor of one boycotted Collegiate Network publication had contacts at the college radio station and the city newspaper, and he convinced both mediums to publicize his case. Draw up a battle plan listing every approach you can take. Then get to your advertisers with that list and show them what you're doing. If they are uneasy about continuing to advertise, encourage them to delay their decisions for a few days while you launch your counteroffensive. And bombard as many of your advertisers as you can with patrons. Support them with your feet. Arrange to patronize all of your big accounts—especially record stores, restaurants, and bars—and take as many of your friends as you can each time.

While this is going on, you may get phone calls from people in your area who support your publication and want to know what they can do to help. Say, "Well, we're probably going to lose some advertisers, and we won't be able to print unless we get some contributions to make up for our losses. Could you help?" Get pledges and the names of others who would be willing to contribute. Send an appeal letter immediately if you have a mailing list of donors and prospective donors. And be sure to call the Collegiate Network for help in publicizing your case. One publication lost all of its advertisers during a boycott, but recovered fully thanks to donations from supporters. Boycotts can be win-win situations, but you have to make a good case to the public when they arise. Your best defense is being able to show that the boycott was the other side's mistake—not yours.

## THREATS

*We've been using university computers to do our typesetting. We don't get special privileges; our staff waits in line to use the computers and printers like everyone else. But somebody reported on us and now this administrator has called us to threaten legal action if we don't stop using public facilities to serve our "right-wing agenda," his exact words. We can't afford our own equipment, so what do we do?*

*One of our editors wrote a piece on affirmative action for our last issue. The black students' organization retaliated by bringing up the article at the last meeting of the faculty-student committee on racial sensitivity. The committee has the power to suspend this editor from school, and I don't exactly see many of our friends on the committee. How do we get out of this mess?*

*I came home last night to find three death threats on my answering machine. I think it had something to do with a story in yesterday's issue. Are these guys serious?*

First of all, relax. Of all the problems that can afflict alternative journalists, direct threats are the problem that has been handled with the highest rate of success. The reason is simple: your opponents are usually smart enough to avoid saying blatantly that they want to shut you down. Instead they rely on means such as those listed above—boycotts, allegations, and more subtle intimidations, like the professor versus the student. Still, the people who threaten you with legal action or school suspension are not dumb. You must react intelligently to their tactics.

When an administrator or student government threatens your publication, you should hold a staff meeting immediately. Tell everyone to keep quiet and direct all press inquiries to the editor in chief. Next, call the CN. Third, get legal help. If you don't have a *pro bono* attorney helping you yet, now is a good time to find one. The CN can be of assistance in finding one. The attorney's role will be to advise you legally, not to steer you into legal conflict. The school will react strongly to any court case you bring against it, and besides, a lawsuit will slow you down a lot more than it will your opponents. Your job right now is not to be vindicated, but to dodge the bullet.

So be pragmatic. *If you stop publishing, the other side wins.* Do everything with the intent of continuing to publish. Make your case strongly in the pages of your publication while you negotiate more cautiously with administrators. Don't submit to following "special guidelines" in order to keep your privileges, like paying a fee to use the school's computers. This is a double standard. Reject it.

Successfully negotiating with administrators requires doing homework first. Read carefully all the student codes thrown at you. Make sure you haven't violated them. Be aware that private colleges and universities are not bound by the Constitution. If they feel certain discourse is destructive to their school, they will quash it. Provided you have not violated the letter of any of these codes, point out their vagueness and argue that these codes don't implicate you. Prepare yourself in advance to meet every attack that may be leveled against you.

One way to ensure as sweet a victory as possible is to put the

Boycott Publicity Machine in action, as explained in the previous section. You will be in good company. As James Meigs reports, "Conservative editors can be tireless when it comes to rallying potential supporters and the national press to their cause. After all, they have an irresistible story: *Valiant student editors battle for free speech.*"

As for death threats, to the best of our knowledge, not one has been carried out. Just to be on the safe side, however, should you or any of your staff receive one, call the campus police immediately. Then call the dean of students. The campus police will advise you about protecting yourself, getting a wiretap on your phone, etc. And remember to get the threat on the public record in your next issue. When a *Northwestern Review* writer was bombarded with death threats after writing an editorial questioning the appropriateness of the Martin Luther King holiday, the *Review* editor assigned a nonpolitical feature writer to do the story. In fact, the writer's tone indicated sympathy for the holiday. But at the heart of his story were the threats, which were roundly condemned by both sides of the King controversy. That story, combined with a full page of letters to the editor, purged the original debate of its fury while exposing a peripheral aspect that had raised its ugly head. It gained sympathy for the publication as a result.

## Declaration of Independence

*A donor who has given $1,000 to our publication wrote us an angry letter the other day about an article we had published on abortion. This donor is generally conservative, but he doesn't like our strong pro-life stand. None of us agrees with the donor, but we don't want to lose him. Besides, he knows several other donors to our publication, and we're afraid he'll call them and tell them to cut us off if we don't appease him. But why should we support a point of view that is identical with our competition's?*

*Well, we took your advice and formed our newspaper separately from the conservative student organization on our campus. Now guess what's happening? They're attacking us for not being conservative! One of the group's leaders even wrote a*

*column in the daily newspaper criticizing us for including too
many feature stories in our publication and for not writing more
editorials about the fall of world communism, abortion, and the
president's domestic policy. We're uncomfortable having to get
into a fight with them because we think it would hurt the
conservative movement here. Should we just keep our mouths
shut?*

The above cases are textbook examples of "when the enemy
of your enemy isn't necessarily your friend." In both cases, of
course, the people causing headaches for you are your friends,
and you want to preserve your friendship with them. At the
same time, situations like these give you pause to reflect on the
fact that you are truly an independent publication, and that
sometimes you must assert your independence. In dealing with
the angry donor, for instance, you not only need to be sensitive
to his demands, but should at the same time be ready to defend
what your publication prints: to stand by your beliefs and your
efforts to reach a large readership to convey those beliefs.
Figuring out the right response to each donor depends in large
part upon how important it is to keep him happy. If your angry
donor is in fact a mere $25 subscriber you may not be able to
accommodate his demands. Perhaps you will simply print his
letter (or, if the donor calls you on the phone, tell him to write a
letter for publication) and leave it at that. On the other hand,
you would want to compromise considerably in order to keep a
well-connected major contributor.

The case of the argumentative conservative who isn't connected with your publication is less troublesome. One response
is to extend a standing offer to him to write a guest column
whenever he pleases, subject of course to editing and even
refusal. If that doesn't work, pragmatically decide how important it is to compromise with him. Conservatives are such a
minority at most schools that it really doesn't make sense for
them to be divided. And since your aim is to influence the
*majority* at your school, it can't be of benefit to waste time
trying to appease a powerless minority-within-a-minority.

Not only will student opinion probably vindicate you, there
are advantages to being perceived as an independent publication that can't make all the conservatives happy. You may not be

as unpredictable as the *New Republic,* but you will encourage the act of thinking critically rather than being faithful to a party line. Thus you will find yourself better equipped to defend the good name and repute of your publication against the simplistic charges of your enemies.

Credibility is a loaded term in the journalism industry because so often it's associated with blandness and false "objectivity." But good alternative publications can attain credibility on their campuses while maintaining their critical edge—the combination that guarantees a long life of consistently provocative journalism.

# 7. FOUR ATTITUDES

*"There are two kinds of college newspapers. To reach for a convenient division, there are the papers whose achievement is measured simply by the raw manufacture and delivery of paper, and the service done to the vanity of those whose names appear as bylines and on the masthead; and those other papers which, however erratic their performance, are instantly recognizable as artifacts presented with passion, with pride, and with joy. It is a participation in such an enterprise that gives true satisfaction, bringing together people of sensitivity and depth." — William F. Buckley Jr.*

AT A COLLEGIATE NETWORK training conference in Milwaukee a couple years ago, Thomas Bray, the editorial page editor of the *Detroit News,* spoke to student editors about the purpose of political journalism. Independent publications, he said, should aim to set the tone and the agenda for campus debate. He coined a phrase, "owning the ballpark," to describe the goal. The home team plays ball by the same rules as its opponents. It owns no special privileges on the field; the visiting team has just as much of a chance to win. But the home team owns the ballpark. Bray said that amidst the chaos and absurdity of today's academic climate, independent publications have a golden opportunity to become voices of reason and sanity on their campuses.

Bray's analogy also suggests a team approach to independent student journalism. Only a team whose members all get the chance to contribute and excel can sustain the great challenge of publishing. The faces may change from year to year, but the idea of the "home team" endures. Years later, you will take personal satisfaction in knowing you helped sustain a paper that made so many young writers' and intellectuals' careers possible, including those of students who came after you and whom you never met.

Alas, that time of proud reflection often seems light-years away. There are times when publishing can be a grueling, seemingly unrewarding endeavor. How can you be sure that others will want to assume these chores when you leave? The bad news is you don't know. The good news is that if you keep four basic attitudes in mind, and they are reflected in your work, not only will you increase the likelihood that a new team will be there when your team retires, but your team will have a sense of pride and accomplishment, regardless of what the future holds.

## A Commitment to Growth

CN independent publications are unsteady. The testimony of those who have come and gone from the scene is that what does not grow, perishes. There is no middle ground for the struggling young publication: it must gain ground or expect to lose it all. Editors who lack innovation to find new story ideas and issues for campus debate will wonder why fewer copies of recent issues are picked up. Publishers who do not keep a growing clientele of advertisers and donors will be forced to cut budgets when the old reservoirs suddenly run dry. And editors and publishers who do not constantly recruit new staff will find themselves spending all their time on mundane chores—and hating them more and more—while the publication slowly grinds to a standstill.

## A Competitive Spirit

Keep asking the question: What can our publication provide to readers and advertisers that our competition doesn't? Know your *raison d'être*, but also know that the future of your mission depends on your ability to publish a better newspaper or magazine than the establishment does. That will be your best defense when you are faced with the accusations of your friends and professors.

## A Pragmatic Spirit

Disagreements inevitably spring up among those on your staff with different ideas about the direction the publication.

Don't let these fester into actual divisions on your staff. Aim to be unified in purpose as much as possible. Resolve internal divisions through compromise, because staff rivalries can be the death of any volunteer organization. If staff members have conflicting views on some of the hot issues of the day, print both views. Let your publication be a ballpark in which opposing staff sides can square off with civility.

## A Commitment to the Future

As hard as you work to instill excellence in your product, work to ensure that you recruit and train like-minded successors. If the next leadership team can start the fall semester with roughly the same level of competence and knowledge that you now have, the publication's growth can continue smoothly, right where your team left off. Transition involves passing on not only technical information, but also the credo and original goals of your publication, year after year.

# EPILOGUE: THE BATTLE OF IDEAS ON AMERICA'S CAMPUSES

*The following remarks were given in March 1983 by Midge Decter of* Commentary *magazine, at the first national conference for the Collegiate Network, cosponsored with the* American Spectator, *in New York City. Her words, a product inevitably of historical context, nonetheless speak to contemporary student editors with such a freshness and relevance that it is as though the words were set to paper today.—Stanley K. Ridgley.*

IT IS MY SPECIAL PRIVILEGE as the first speaker at today's conference to welcome you all to the war of ideas. For that, of course, is the name of the enterprise that you have all, knowingly or unknowingly, signed on for. As students, you do not have to be told the importance of ideas: they are, so to speak, the way you are currently making your living. They are also the way the rest of us in this room one way or another are making *our* living. Nevertheless, before I tell you something about the order of battle—at least as we see it—I want to say something about these ideas that we are engaged in a common war over.

Ideas and the study of ideas and the transmission of ideas rule the world. As we learned from the Tet offensive during the Vietnam War, for instance, even so hard and material thing as a military victory is not a military victory if those who report on it refuse to say so. I do not have to tell you how one battles against bad and false ideas. Your presence here today betokens the fact that you know how as well as I. By a constant, unremitting, and hopefully cheerful effort to replace these ideas in the minds of reasonable people. I shall come back to that word *cheerful.*

Your presence here today also betokens the fact that you are people with literary or journalistic or publicist ambitions. There are many ways to get into the fight to break the dominance of America-hating attitudes that has driven you to find some alternative for yourselves. The way you have chosen, through publication, says certain things about you—at least about most of you.

People who write and transmit their thoughts through print are for the most part not the same kind of people who express themselves through organizational activism. Your demonstrations are for the most part the demonstrations of argument. You will, for the most part again, find yourselves the indispensable allies of those who do march. I propose no hierarchy here of which is the more important. There can be no change of policies in this country without elections; but equally, as the people who reposed such hopes in the election of Ronald Reagan have recently learned, no matter who is elected or to what, there can be no change of policies unless and until there is a change in the climate of opinion. That is where you, and we, all of us, come in.

Since I have presumed, on the basis of an experience rather longer than yours, to welcome you to our battle, I want also to presume to tell you what you might expect to find on the front.

A word first about war aims. You will not convert the foe to your cause. Nor will you, in the university, overcome him with superior might—no matter what you do. Your purpose, like ours, is to raise a standard and clear the ground, the ground on which others, too timid to speak up or too unsure to undergo the discomforts of rising above the crowd, will be able to stand.

One of the thoughts about this battle that is, alas, far too widely held and that is in my opinion a crippling one, is that it is a waste of time, as people put it, to "preach to the converted." Any successful leader will tell you that it is to the converted, precisely, that you must preach. Because a leader's task is twofold: to provide the ideas and the language behind which his supporters can know they have a clear field, and—*and*—to, *put heart in them.*

Am I saying that you should be quite ideologically narrow? The answer is yes, provided that you understand the word *ideological* to be a framework, a boundary, a set of common assumptions. Debates between and among people who are in fundamental agreement and disagree on detail can be fruitful, enlightening, and also energizing. Debates between and among people who cannot agree about a, b, c are sterile contests. You learn nothing from them except who was on some particular occasion cleverer than whom.

The whole of your enterprise is a debate—with people who deny the fundamental principles in which you believe. You will know you have struck blows in *that* debate not when your opponents grow silent—for they never will—but when in fact they grow more noisy—for that will mean that you have drawn blood.

The important thing to remember is that you are in a minority. Not, paradoxically, a minority of the American people but a minority of the community in which you find yourselves, the community of the university, and of the community in which you are most likely to find yourselves on leaving the university, that is, the community of the educated professional elite. As members of a minority, you will be burdened with what you might think of as an unfair responsibility: you will have to do better than the other guys in order to be considered as good.

They can call on unthinking pieties; you will have to think, think hard and well.

They can circulate lies; you will have to counter with the truth, and the truth is always more complicated and demanding than lies.

They can say the words "El Salvador," for instance, and depend on a whole, already established, false frame of reference; you will have to marshal strong and persuasive argument. It will do you no good to rail against this double standard; that is the way it is. On the other hand, the fact that a double standard will be applied to you is also one of your greatest strengths, if you let it be.

For the business of journalism, even literary journalism, even poetry magazines—on campus and off—is to attract attention. That is the name of the game, even as between *Time* and *Newsweek,* and the *New York Times* and the *Washington Post.* Attention is a shortage commodity. When you go for it you are necessarily in competition with others; you have to *earn* it. And the need to be better will make you more lively. If you publish fiction, it has to be better fiction. If you publish reviews, they have to be more trenchant reviews. If your chosen mode is to poke fun at the opposition—and it can be a powerful mode indeed—it has to be done well. It has to hit its target accurately. If you say to yourself, "My side is the side of virtue; that is a sufficient standard for me," you're dead.

In all of this, you have a great advantage right now. The other side is choking on its political and social conventionality. The fresh talent, the new thoughts, the intelligence, and the energy are with *you.*

There is another responsibility that will come, if it has not already, to devolve upon you. I don't know how better to describe this responsibility than to say that you will be providing a home for people. Magazines, while not, as I said, activist enterprises, have their nature—they are not movements, not even clubs, and of their essence they are undemocratic. Nevertheless, good magazines tend to become social centers. They collect people—writers, readers—probably because they are a collective voice. In any case, you will be doing more than consigning words to print; you will be defining a crowd, a gang. The more your time is wasted and your patience called upon, in negotiating your way among a variety of delicate personalities, the more successful you can account yourselves.

But your experience is going to try your characters in many more departments than that of patience, and many more important ones. Being in fights is for all but a very few people an unpleasant and often frightening experience. Name-calling is one of the chief and most time-honored weapons of the Left; ditto for distortion and twisting your words. Many times you will have the impulse to say, "But I'm really a nice person. Why am I being likened to Hitler, or why am I being held responsible for torture in Chilean prisons?" Many times you will find yourself surrounded by people, friends, whose moral support will consist of the statement, "But *you* don't really care what anybody says about you." These will be critical moments for you, intellectually as well as spiritually. For no matter how you feel, you will have to remember that it is people who have no arguments to offer who resort to insult and outrage. In other words, you will be facing bullies. They wish to silence you.

There has in fact been a tremendous campaign of this sort to silence us all. Understand that like all campaigns undertaken by bullies, it is a campaign based on fear. How do you answer? How do you, for instance if you are an opponent of the freeze, answer the charge that you are looking forward with joy to a nuclear war? Or if you are an opponent of women's lib, that you believe in the inferiority of women? Or if an opponent of affirmative action, that you are a racist? If you remain silent, you grant those who would silence you a victory.

If you defend yourself, by which I mean denying these charges with the claim that you are so too a feeling and caring person, you have once again ceded the ground by affirming the relevance, if not the substance, of the charge. There is only one thing to do: press the argument; if possible, make it even better the second time. If you cannot be bullied, not only your opponent but you yourself will taste your strength.

Which brings me to the last thing I want to say to you. You may feel the picture I have painted of what you have got yourselves into is not a pretty one. I suppose in some respects it's not. But what I have not said—and what you have all surely experienced by now—is how much fun all this is. I mean *fun* in the very highest sense: of being energized, entertained, and uplifted by what one is doing. You are surrounded by people who, either irresponsibly or intentionally, seek to bring this blessed country down, and you and your future children with it. Instead of sitting around and cursing your fate, you are lending your best strength and talent to the collective struggle to break their influence.

Early in this talk I used the word *cheerful*. Nothing is more cheering than to speak one's mind openly and clearly. And nothing will better accomplish our end, yours and mine, and put our opponents more permanently out of countenance, than the sight of us all going about our business with good cheer, in high spirits. You and I have been afforded the opportunity to do just that. For that, we should all be grateful.

# Appendix:
# How to Write a
# Grant Proposal
# to the Collegiate
# Network

ONCE EACH YEAR all Collegiate Network member publications seeking financial support must submit a proposal to the CN. Once you are a member of the Collegiate Network, you are eligible to submit a proposal.

The annual deadline, usually May 1, is posted in *Newslink* and on the editors' internet discussion group well in advance, so you have time to prepare. We encourage you to gather information and begin writing your proposal well before the crunch of finals absorbs all of your time.

Writing the proposal doesn't have to be a chore. In fact, think of it as writing a letter to a friend or an informative article for your paper. We want to know certain information about your paper: What issues have crystallized on campus as focal points of contention? Who are your staff members and what are their academic majors and other interests? What are your paper's goals for the coming year?

One of the most important things you can do to ensure continuity from year to year is to craft, publicize, and maintain a mission statement for your paper. Your paper's statement of purpose tells us and other interested parties what you stand for. We look forward to reading that statement.

Please submit your grant request in a timely manner. Meeting deadlines is an indicator of a staff's seriousness of purpose, so we evaluate first all requests that are received by the deadline. After we have considered and processed those requests, we then look at late requests and administer any remaining funds. It pays to be prompt.

Here are eleven suggestions for writing good proposals:

*1. Tell us the history of your publication.* Emphasize recent events. What successes and failures have you experienced so far this year? What are your immediate and long-term goals, in terms of both staff organization and story content?

*2. Describe the impact your publication makes on campus.* Do you bring important issues to the attention of students, faculty, administrators, and trustees? How do students react to each issue, and how much serious attention do your ideas get?

*3. Introduce us to key people on your staff.* List their positions, their class years, and academic majors; and tell us their contributions to the publication. Include a brief note about recruiting success: how many freshmen and sophomores are on your staff?

*4. Explain why your paper needs the money.* In other words, tell us why advertising, subscription, and donor revenues will not meet your budget needs. If you've attempted fundraising, explain what it was and how much it brought (and why it wasn't enough). How will you attempt to raise more next term?

*5. Include a line-item budget.* Show all expense items in one column, all projected revenue items in a second column. The difference should be the amount of your request. You don't have to get this down to the penny, but you should have a good idea of what printing, mailing, production, and other items cost.

*6. Ask for a sum we are likely to give.* The CN makes grants for operating expenses only; we do not fund capital purchases such as computer equipment or software. We do not fund salaries.

*7. Ask for a sum that you really need.* Unlike a government agency, the CN does not arbitrarily subtract 5 or 10 percent just for the sake of doing so. We assume your request is exactly the amount you need.

*8. Write well!* We support publications that pay attention to the quality of their ideas and their writing. Have plenty of both in your grant proposal. Besides, good proposals can be adapted for use in soliciting donations from other private sources such as alumni, parents, and prominent local conservatives.

*9. Conclude by looking forward.* Summarize your goals and future financial needs. How will our grant affect your paper?

*10. Get the proposal here on time.* We don't even look at late proposals until we've completed those that arrived on time.

*11. If you're unsure, ask us.* CN student publications are sometimes prey for outside groups with messages that can be unsavory. What may sound like good advice or "technique" or a "freedom of speech" issue can turn out to be the opposite. Be aware of this and remember that the CN is the nation's clearinghouse for reliable information on the college conservative press. The best advice about college conservative journalism comes from the Home of College Conservative Journalism—the Collegiate Network—so give us a call or e-mail.

If you have any other questions about submitting a grant proposal, contact us at the Collegiate Network—(800) 225-2862 or at cn@isi.org.

# INDEX

## A NOTE ON THE TYPE

This book was set in Optima, a san serif typeface designed in the 1950s by one of the twentieth century's geniuses of typography, Hermann Zapf. Modern, yet classic in appearance, Optima is unusual among sans serifs in that it maintains the stroke/weight variations more commonly found in serif typefaces.